A LIFE OBSERVED

A LIFE OBSERVED

A Spiritual Biography
of C. S. Lewis

DEVIN BROWN

BrazosPress
a division of Baker Publishing Group
Grand Rapids, Michigan

Published by Brazos Press
a division of Baker Publishing Group
P.O. Box 6287, Grand Rapids, MI 49516-6287
www.brazospress.com

Printed in the United States of America

Library of Congress Cataloging-in-Publication Data
Brown, Devin.
    A life observed : a spiritual biography of C. S. Lewis / Devin Brown.
        pages cm
    Includes bibliographical references and index.
    ISBN 978-1-58743-335-1 (pbk.)
    1. Lewis, C. S. (Clive Staples), 1898–1963—Religion. 2. Christian literature, English—History and criticism. I. Title.
    BX5199.L53B76 2013
    230′.092—dc23   2013007334

13   14   15   16   17   18   19   7   6   5   4   3   2   1

In memory of my father,
whose work as an electrician
paid for all those books
I grew up loving

Contents

Foreword

It takes a confident man to write a biography of C. S. Lewis and then turn to me for comments. After all, there have been many biographies of Jack already written, including the one I wrote for children. I have said often enough that they vary from the good to the bad to the just plain ugly. Biographies are written for a variety of reasons, and these too vary in the same way: some are written to advance knowledge of the subject and his or her work; others, to advance the biographer in fame and fortune; and still others are little more than attempts to leap on a passing bandwagon. But the biography that follows is different. It has a better, more valuable reason for its existence.

I have more or less given up reading the new biographies of Jack, not so much because of the inaccuracies they contain—though there are usually enough of them—but because they are written by people who knew him far less well than I did, if they knew him at all. Their words, speaking only of the good biographies, are the products of much reading of Jack's works and much research into what others have written about him. They are consequently prone not only to error but also to a more serious malady—they dry out! The pages crackle with facts, faces, places, dates, and history. Some of them are very good books *about* Jack, but—here's the rub—Jack is not in them.

But this book is different. It is the story of Jack's real and true life—not the mere flash of the firefly in the infinite darkness of time that is our momentary life in this world, but the one he left this world to begin—and how he came to attain it. Brown helpfully works his way through the dross and difficulties of Jack's earthly life in search of every factor, every influence, every event, and all of the people who showed Jack where the narrow path lay and taught him where it led.

I am the only person now living who lived with Jack in his home and grew to know him very well. I am the only person alive who watched as Jack wept with the pain of a crippling illness and yet smiled at me, saying that it was just something to be borne with fortitude and "is probably very good for me." I grew up with Jack as my guide. This real Jack whom I knew walks the pages of this book.

Douglas Gresham
Malta, February 2013

Preface

There is a kind of C. S. Lewis biography which is lengthy and definitive. In it readers find out when Lewis's great-great-grandfather was born and what Richard Lewis, for that was his name, did for a living.

This is not that kind of biography.

Anyone who sets out to write a new book about a famous person should do so only because either (a) some new source of information has become available or (b) the author takes a new approach. My justification for *A Life Observed: A Spiritual Biography of C. S. Lewis* is the latter.

While other biographers have provided excellent comprehensive, broad-ranging accounts of the events—large and small—which surrounded Lewis's life, my goal is to focus closely on the story of Lewis's spiritual journey and his search for the object of the mysterious longing he called Joy (always capitalized), a quest which he claimed was the central story of his life.

In *Mere Christianity* Lewis concentrated on the key aspects of the Christian faith. My focus in this biography could be described as *Mere C. S. Lewis*. My hope is to provide a concise introduction to Lewis and his best-known works for a new generation of readers, a generation who may know him only through the Narnia films.

In the preface to his autobiography, *Surprised by Joy*, Lewis cautions that how far the story matters to anyone but himself will depend on the degree to which they, too, have experienced the special longing he calls Joy. He finishes the preface with this declaration: "I have tried to so write the first chapter that those who can't bear such a story will see at once what they are in for and close the book with the least waste of time" (viii).

I can do no better than to echo this statement in my own preface.

Before starting, I have a few words of housekeeping. When quoting from other sources, I indicate the author or the work within the text. After the quote, I give the page number in parentheses. Readers who wish to look up a quotation can find the source in the bibliography. To keep citations to a minimum, whenever I have two or more quotes in the same paragraph from the same page of any source, I include the page number only after the first quotation. I have used Americanized spellings and have written out any words that were abbreviated.

I have needed to use a few abbreviations of my own. To indicate quotations from the recently published three-volume set *The Collected Letters of C. S. Lewis*, I use the abbreviations *CLI*, *CLII*, and *CLIII*. With quotations from the unpublished *Lewis Papers* at the Wade Center at Wheaton College, I use the abbreviation *LP*. In addition, all references to Lewis's diary come from *All My Road Before Me: The Diary of C. S. Lewis, 1922–1927*. References to the diary of Warren Lewis come from *Brothers and Friends: The Diaries of Major Warren Hamilton Lewis*. Information on these works can be found in the bibliography at the end of this book.

In a letter written as he was nearing the completion of his monumental work *English Literature in the Sixteenth Century*,

Excluding Drama, Lewis confesses that he was afraid of hidden errors, for unlike a mistake in a laboratory experiment which immediately makes itself known, a literary mistake exists in silence "till the day it turns irrevocable in a printed book and the book goes for review to the only man in England who would have known it was a mistake" (*CLIII*, 149–50). A number of people deserve thanks for helping answer my questions and correct my mistakes. They include David Downing, Alan Jacobs, Peter Schakel, Laura Schmidt, Phil Tallon, Heidi Truty, Michael Ward, the Reverend Tim Stead, and the staffs of St. Mark's Church in Belfast and Holy Trinity Church in Headington. I want to especially thank Karen Koehn, Marv Hinten, Richard James, and Richard Platt for their extensive comments, insights, and encouragement. In addition, I would like to express my deep appreciation to Douglas Gresham for his help in making my portrait of Jack more accurate.

Prologue

A Longing Nothing Can Satisfy

If I find in myself a desire which no experience in this
world can satisfy, the most probable explanation is that
I was made for another world.

—*Mere Christianity*, book 3, chapter 10

Introduction

At around four in the afternoon, on November 22, 1963, Warren
Hamilton Lewis carried tea to the small downstairs bedroom of
his home in the quiet English suburbs. He was glad to see that
his younger brother, who had been in poor health for several
months, was resting comfortably, though very drowsy. Major
Lewis—Major because he had served in the British Armed Forces
in both World War I and World War II, but known to everyone

as simply Warnie—was sixty-eight. His brother was a week short of turning sixty-five.

The few words they exchanged were to be their last.

At five thirty, Warnie heard a sound and rushed in to find his brother lying unconscious at the foot of his bed. A few minutes later, Clive Staples Lewis—or Jack, as he was known to his friends and family—ceased breathing.

Today—fifty years after his quiet death in the brothers' modest house just outside of Oxford—the man who many have called the most influential Christian writer of our times continues to live on in the books he left behind, continues to challenge and inspire. And the story of C. S. Lewis's life—his journey from cynical atheism to joyous Christianity, his remarkable friendship with J. R. R. Tolkien, the legendary meetings with the writing group known as the Inklings, and his experience of deep love and deep heartbreak late in life—is as fascinating and as moving as any of the stories he wrote.

The Experience of "Joy"

As his fame as a writer spread, C. S. Lewis soon began receiving requests to recount the story of his spiritual journey, to tell how it was that he went from being a committed skeptic to being a committed Christian. Finally, in response to these appeals, in the late 1940s Lewis began a modest-length autobiographical work describing his life up to his conversion. Due to intervening work on *English Literature in the Sixteenth Century* and the Chronicles of Narnia, *Surprised by Joy: The Shape of My Early Life* was not published until some seven or eight years later, in September 1955, when Lewis was fifty-six years old.

One of the first things that Lewis makes clear in his autobiography is that by *Joy*—which Lewis spells with a capital *J*—he does not mean *joy* in the normal sense of gladness or elation.

He is using the word only because he cannot find a better one—at least not in English. At the very start of the story of his conversion, Lewis defines *Joy* to mean a special kind of intense longing he felt, beginning in childhood, for something he could not quite put his finger on.

Of course, it was a sensation of desire; but a desire for what? Lewis wonders. "Before I knew what I desired, the desire itself was gone, the whole glimpse withdrawn, the world turned commonplace again" (16).

Although he did not know what this desire was for or where it came from, Lewis knew one thing: it was very powerful, so much so that he confesses to us that he finds it difficult to come up with words strong enough to describe it. One thing he can tell us is that anyone who has experienced it will want it again. There is bliss in this deep longing, he explains. It is also colored by a feeling of sadness or sorrow, but this sadness is a kind that we want.

Lewis took his title, *Surprised by Joy*, from a sonnet by the English poet William Wordsworth which begins with these two lines:

> Surprised by joy—impatient as the wind
> I turned to share the transport

Lewis uses Wordsworth's first line on the title page of *Surprised by Joy* as an epigraph for the book. Like the wind, this Joy would come and go in Lewis's life as it wished, sometimes appearing regularly, other times disappearing for long periods. When it did come, its presence was always fleeting, or as the sonnet says, impatient. But rather than leaving him sorrowful or distraught with its departure, the momentary experience left Lewis troubled, to his lifelong enrichment, with a dim sense of something that hovered just beyond what his consciousness could grasp—something unattainable but wonderful. He described this Joy that surprised him now and again as an unsatisfied desire which was more desirable than any other satisfaction.

In chapter 1 of his autobiography, Lewis concludes his initial description of this mysterious desire with an explicit warning, making it clear that if readers are not interested in the questions of what this strange longing was and where it came from, they need read no further. Why the warning? "The central story of my life is about nothing else," Lewis explains (17).

The central story of my life is about nothing else. In chapter 10 of *The Problem of Pain*, a work published in 1940, relatively early in Lewis's writing career, we find one of his most moving attempts to articulate what he meant by this experience of Joy.

> You may have noticed that the books you really love are bound together by a secret thread. You know very well what is the common quality that makes you love them, though you cannot put it into words. . . . You have stood before some landscape, which seems to embody what you have been looking for all your life. . . . Even in your hobbies, has there not always been some secret attraction . . . , the smell of cut wood in the workshop or the clap-clap of water against the boat's side? . . . That something which you were born desiring, and which beneath the flux of other desires and in all the momentary silences between the louder passions, night and day, year by year from childhood to old age, you are looking for, watching for, listening for. (130)

After pointing out various ways this deep longing may come to us—through cherished books, certain landscapes, and favorite hobbies—Lewis takes the next step, maintaining that none of these contain the true object of our desire. They are only the vehicles this special longing may come through.

"You have never *had* it," Lewis writes (131). He goes on to explain that all of the things that have ever deeply possessed our souls have been but hints of it.

> Tantalizing glimpses, promises never quite fulfilled, echoes that died away just as they caught your ear. But if it should really

become manifest—if there ever came an echo that did not die away but swelled into the sound itself—you would know it. Beyond all possibility of doubt you would say, "Here at last is the thing I was made for."

Lewis tells us that his life's central story is about nothing else. But his use of an all-inclusive *you* here in these passages—though *you* cannot put it into words . . . that something which *you* were born desiring . . . *you* have never had it . . . *you* would know it—makes it clear that Lewis believes this is a longing we all have felt.

Lewis might say this is the central story of everyone's life.

Lewis came to identify this longing—which haunted and disturbed him, in the best sense, down through the years—as a longing for heaven, our true home. At the end of *The Last Battle*, Lewis has Jewel the Unicorn give voice to these thoughts. Upon reaching the new Narnia, Jewel declares: "I have come home at last! This is my real country! I belong here. This is the land I have been looking for all my life, though I never knew it till now" (196).

But we are getting ahead of ourselves.

If, as Lewis claimed, the central story of his life was his search for the object of this deep longing, then it makes sense also to make it the central story of a biography such as this one and to follow Lewis's quest for the source of this mysterious Joy to its journey's end.

This, then, is the story of Lewis's quest to find his real country. And in Lewis's quest, we may see reflected aspects of our own.

An Atheist Is Surprised

When Lewis tells us that he was surprised by Joy, surprised to find in himself a desire which nothing in this world could satisfy, he was surprised because, as a fervent materialist who believed the physical world was all there is, he felt that this longing *should not exist.*

During Lewis's time, perhaps more so than today, there were a good number of writers and thinkers who might be called, for lack of a better term, *reluctant* atheists. After having been raised in the simple faith of their childhood, they would go off to the university and encounter the great minds of their day or, alternatively, to the battlefield and encounter the great horrors of their day, and these experiences would initiate a process that led them to the conclusion that the Christian story of a loving Father in heaven who sent his Son to save the world was only a fairy tale, something previous generations had made up long ago to help them feel better about their place in a frightening and meaningless universe. But rather than despising their childhood faith, these reluctant atheists then spent the rest of their days in melancholy, viewing their loss of faith with sadness and wishing that somehow they could still believe.

We meet one of these reluctant atheists in Matthew Arnold's famous poem "Dover Beach." There the speaker in the poem laments the retreat of the sea of faith and points out how bleak and bare he finds the world it has left behind.

We see a similar reluctant atheism in the narrator of Thomas Hardy's poem "The Oxen," who expresses nostalgia for the comforting, unsophisticated beliefs of his youth, a faith he no longer is able to embrace. In the final line, he reports that if invited to go see the miracle of the kneeling oxen on Christmas Eve, he would go in the gloom, hoping it might be so. But this gloom is far deeper than just the darkness of nighttime, and hoping here means the kind of wishing that knows, and regrets, that it will be otherwise.

The purpose in describing these reluctant atheists is simply to point out that Lewis was not one of them. In chapter 11 of *Surprised by Joy*, Lewis writes that a godless, materialistic universe held out one great attraction to him: freedom from what he called the "transcendental Interferer" (172). For much of Lewis's life, his most persistent wish when it came to God was a strong desire to be left alone. In this way his atheism, begun in earnest when he was around fourteen and lasting until around the time he turned thirty, was a great relief, not something he regretted.

Since Lewis was not a reluctant atheist but an enthusiastic and often arrogant one, we might go so far as to say that he was not only surprised by this Joy he experienced but also shocked by it. What origins could feelings like this have, and what purpose, for someone who so wholeheartedly embraced materialism?

In *Mere Christianity* Lewis makes the following proposition: "Creatures are not born with desires unless satisfaction for those desires exists" (136). He then gives us several illustrations of this principle: Babies get hungry, and there is such a thing as food to satisfy this hunger. Ducklings want to swim, and there is such a thing as water. Humans feel sexual longing, and for this desire there is sex.

If, as Lewis believed until around the midpoint of his life, there is nothing beyond nature—nothing beyond what we can see, touch, taste, and smell—then where, Lewis asked, *did this longing that nothing in this world could satisfy come from*?

Toward the middle of *Surprised by Joy*, Lewis comments, "I was at this time living, like so many Atheists . . . in a whirl of contradictions" (115). A thoroughgoing materialist who felt an unearthly longing—this paradox is at the heart of his story.

Infant and Child

(1 8 9 8 – 1 9 0 8)

And every day there were what we called "the Green
Hills"; that is, the low line of the Castlereagh Hills
which we saw from the nursery windows. They were
not very far off but they were, to children, quite unattainable. They taught me longing.

—*Surprised by Joy*, chapter 1

Belfast, 1898

Near the middle of chapter 7 of *The Magician's Nephew*, we
find a striking illustration that shows Jadis, the future White
Witch of Narnia, straddling the roof of a horse-drawn cab, the
reins in one hand, a whip in the other. The hansom, which is

barreling down a brick-paved street and about to crash into a gas streetlight, belongs to Frank, a working-class cabby and the future King Frank. In a second illustration that follows two pages later, we see the crowd which the mayhem has drawn: policemen with their old-fashioned bobby uniforms and nightsticks, errand boys on bicycles, the newspaper boy, the butcher's boy, and clusters of butlers and housemaids.

Both of these illustrations show us Great Britain at the turn of the century.

This time period, which seems almost a fairy tale setting to us today—the time of Peter Pan and Sherlock Holmes—was a time Lewis knew not from books but because it was the world he was born into. For Lewis, this world of horse travel, gas lights, brick-lined streets, and maids and butlers was not a fictional world, nor the world of previous generations, but his world, the world of his youth.

Clive Staples Lewis was born near the end of Queen Victoria's long reign in the final years of the nineteenth century, on November 29, 1898. In some ways the world he was born into resembled the world of the Middle Ages more than it does our world today.

Picture a world before space shuttles, airplanes, cars, or buses, a world where the vast majority of travel on land was done by foot, on horseback, or in a carriage or cart pulled by an animal. A world without the internet, cell phones, television, or even the radio. A world nearly everywhere still lit only by fire. Not only were there no computers—desktops, laptops, or tablets—to write with in 1898, but there were also no ballpoint pens. During Lewis's lifetime the fountain pen—a nib pen with an ink reservoir in the handle—would become widely available, but except for a relatively short time during his years as an undergraduate at Oxford, Lewis never used one.

Picture Lewis as a child, learning to write with a pen he had to dip into his inkpot every four or five words to refill. Except for the metal point of the nib, his method of writing—a method used till the end of his life, during which he literally penned thirty-eight books, over two hundred essays, and thousands of letters—was more similar to that of a medieval monk copying manuscripts with a quill than today's modern methods.

It should not really surprise us that Lewis sometimes may sound a bit dated—as he does, for example, when he has Peter and Edmund go around exclaiming "By Jove!" in the Narnia books. What is amazing is how current he remains after five decades, and even prophetic, addressing such topics as cruelty to animals, women's body image, and the postmodern denial of absolute truth long before they became current.

In one way Belfast could be said to have regressed since 1898. During Lewis's youth, Belfast was not just a thriving industrial city but also the world's greatest shipyard. While today efforts are being made to reclaim its former glory, modern Belfast cannot match the golden age of manufacturing Lewis witnessed as a boy.

In the opening chapter of *Surprised by Joy*, Lewis describes the view of Belfast Lough—the site where the RMS *Titanic* was built. Lewis tells us that the story of his life begins in the "far-off days when Britain was the world's carrier and the Lough was full of shipping" (11). He goes on to note that even when he was in his fifties, the sound of a ship's horn in the night still evoked the distant memories of his boyhood.

Lewis was born in Belfast, *Ireland*—not Northern Ireland, as the region is called now—because in 1898 the island had not yet been partitioned into the Irish Republic in the south and the six-county region to the north that alone has remained a part of the UK. In one way modern-day Belfast still resembles the Belfast that Lewis was born into: strong divisions between Catholics and Protestants remain—although the hostility between the two factions has lessened. In chapter 14 of *Surprised by Joy*, Lewis, who came from a Protestant family, tells of his first meeting with J. R. R. Tolkien, who was Roman Catholic, noting, "At my first coming into the world I had been (implicitly) warned never to trust a Papist" (216). Perhaps because of the firsthand exposure to the "Troubles" between Catholics and Protestants in his childhood, later in life Lewis would write *Mere Christianity*, a work in which he intentionally put forth the beliefs which *all* Christians at all times have believed, and would speak out strongly against the divisions that continue to plague the Christian faith.

Besides the ongoing antagonism between its Christian factions, there is yet another way that modern-day Belfast resembles the Belfast of 1898, and this is the weather. As we will see, the inclement Irish weather featured prominently in the story of Lewis's childhood.

St. Mark's

Two physical structures are associated with Lewis's beginnings in Belfast: St. Mark's, the church his family attended (which through its membership in the Church of Ireland was part of the Anglican Communion); and Little Lea, the big house they moved to in 1905. St. Mark's played a relatively small part in Lewis's life. By contrast, Lewis tells us, Little Lea played a critical role, both in his childhood and in the kind of person he would later become.

The baptismal records of St. Mark's Church, located in the Dundela section of Belfast, include an entry for an infant named Clive Staples. This entry tells us the basic facts about the Lewis family.

In the rectangular space for the child's birth date is written "Nov 29 1898." In the space for when baptized, we find "1899 Jan 29." Also recorded is "No 186," indicating that little Clive was the 186th child to have been baptized since the new record book was begun. The first volume went from the church's origins in 1864 to 1889; the second covered 1889 to 1904. In the rectangular space for the parents' Christian names we see "Albert James & Florence Augusta." In the space for the name of the priest who conducted the baptism is written "Thos Hamilton."

The Reverend Thomas Hamilton was Flora Lewis's father, and so Lewis was baptized by his grandfather, who was the vicar of the church. Five years earlier, in 1894, the Reverend Hamilton had presided at the wedding ceremony at St. Mark's for his daughter and Albert. When the couple's first son was born in 1895, Flora's maiden name, Hamilton, was used for Warnie's middle name. Lewis would later use the pen name Clive Hamilton for his first two books of poetry.

The address recorded is "Dundela Villas, Strandtown," the family's first home, one of a pair of semidetached houses where both brothers were born, about two miles from the center of Belfast.

In the rectangular space for "Quality, Trade, or Profession" we find *Solicitor*, Albert's profession. Here, in lieu of employment, the father's "quality" would have been indicated—that is, if he was a gentleman or not. There is no space in this early record book for any similar information about the mother. Flora had graduated with a degree in mathematics from Queen's University, a rarity for the time. Like most married women of her day, she was a mother and homemaker.

If we look back several pages to entry number 108, we find the record of Warnie's baptism a few years before, on July 20, 1895. The large stone font where the brothers were baptized remains in use at the church today. Visitors to the church can see it and the stained glass window of Saints Luke, James, and Mark which Jack and Warnie donated in 1935 in memory of their parents.

Lewis makes it clear that the Christian teachings he was exposed to as a child at St. Mark's made neither a very big nor a very lasting impression on him. In *Surprised by Joy*, Lewis writes that during his youth "religious experiences did not occur at all" (7). He goes on to explain: "I was taught the usual things and made to say my prayers and in due time taken to church. I naturally accepted what I was told but I cannot remember feeling much interest in it."

In a letter dated February 15, 1946, after being asked to give a brief account of his spiritual life, Lewis begins: "I was baptized in the Church of Ireland (same as Anglican). My parents were not notably pious but went regularly to church and took me" (*CLII*, 702).

Lewis says little about his parents' faith and what beliefs they were able to pass on to him, possibly because there is not much to say. As we will see, when Lewis was young, he lost his mother to cancer. In *Surprised by Joy*, he confesses that he can say almost nothing from memory of his mother's religion. About Albert's faith we are given two sentences. In the first, Lewis notes that his father was rather high church and then tells us, "His approach to religion . . . was at the opposite pole from what later became my own" (7–8). In the second sentence Lewis writes that Albert delighted in the "charm of tradition" and the "verbal beauty" of the Bible and the Prayer Book and concludes by saying that it would have been difficult to find someone equally as intelligent as his father who "cared so little for metaphysics" (8).

Parents who were not notably pious but who went regularly to church. A father who loved the tradition and verbal beauty found in the services at St. Mark's but took no interest in metaphysics, and whose approach to religion was the opposite of the one Lewis himself took later in life. In chapter 10 of *Surprised by Joy* Lewis will relate how at age sixteen he was confirmed at St. Mark's and made his first Communion, despite being an atheist at the time in a state of total disbelief. He reports that it would have been impossible to discuss his objections to being confirmed with his father, because Albert's answer to him would not have been based on Jack's lack of belief in the Sacrament itself but instead on "the beauty of the Authorized Version, the beauty of the Christian tradition and sentiment and character" (162).

It might be tempting to try to read between the lines here to find something Lewis does not directly say about the faith of his father. These comments expand his claim that religious experiences played no part in his childhood and that beyond accepting what he was told, he had little connection to matters of faith.

As a young boy, Lewis made several attempts to keep a diary, none very long-lived. Then in 1922, when he was an undergraduate student at Oxford, Lewis started a new diary, which he continued for five years. This diary was made public under the title *All My Road Before Me* in 1991, twenty-eight years after Lewis's death. An entry from this diary, an entry Lewis wrote after his childhood had passed, may offer a window on the kind of conversations Albert had with Jack and Warnie—or, in this case, did not have—about matters of faith.

Jack and Warnie had gone home for Christmas, and in this entry written at Little Lea, dated December 25, 1922, we read:

> We were awakened early by my father to go to the Communion Service. It was a dark morning with a gale blowing and some very cold rain. We tumbled out and got under way. As we walked down to church we started discussing the time of sunrise; my father saying rather absurdly that it must have risen already, or else it wouldn't be light.
>
> In church it was intensely cold. Warnie offered to keep his coat on. My father expostulated and said, "Well at least you won't keep it on when you go up to the Table." Warnie asked

why not and was told it was "most disrespectful." I couldn't help wondering why. But Warnie took it off to save trouble. (158)

While this diary entry belongs to a somewhat later period in his life, in chapter 7 of *Surprised by Joy*, Lewis gives us another glimpse of his strained relationship with his father—particularly concerning spiritual matters. There Lewis explains that while at Wynyard School, a time when he was trying to live as a Christian, he wrote out a set of rules for himself and put them in his pocket. On one of the holiday breaks when Jack returned to Little Lea, his father noticed his pockets bulging with all sorts of papers and, not liking how they pulled his son's coat out of shape, began removing them. "I would have died rather than let him see my list of good resolutions," Lewis writes (120). Somehow without Albert noticing, young Jack managed to slip his list of Christian rules into the fireplace, preferring to burn them before allowing his father to read them.

Two further windows may help to fill out our picture of Lewis's childhood beliefs. The first is a short sentence found in *Letters to an American Lady*. Lewis's correspondent, an elderly widow from Washington, DC, wrote to him worried about a young person whose religious education was being neglected. In a letter dated September 19, 1954, we may hear hints of Lewis's own childhood as he writes, "Remember how much religious education has exactly the opposite effect to that which was intended" (32).

A second window comes from a well-known passage in the essay "Sometimes Fairy Stories May Say Best What's to Be Said," where Lewis explains how he first came to write his famous seven-volume series of fairy tales, the Chronicles of Narnia. There Lewis recounts:

> I thought I saw how stories of this kind could steal past a certain inhibition which had paralyzed much of my own religion in childhood. Why did one find it so hard to feel as one was told

one ought to feel about God or about the sufferings of Christ? I thought the chief reason was that one was told one ought to. An obligation to feel can freeze feelings. And reverence itself did harm. The whole subject was associated with lowered voices, almost as if it were something medical. But supposing that by casting all these things into an imaginary world, stripping them of their stained-glass and Sunday School associations, one could make them for the first time appear in their real potency? (47)

From this passage we can conclude that when Lewis was exposed to the gospel as a child, it was presented to him in a way that did not communicate its true power, its real potency, and so paralyzed his religious development for a long time.

Would Lewis say that as a young person he was a follower of Christ? The answer is not given until later, after he left home to go to boarding school, and then only briefly. He concludes this section about his early spirituality in *Surprised by Joy* by telling us that his childhood was "not in the least other-worldly" (8). Twenty-five pages later, in chapter 2 of *Surprised by Joy*, Lewis describes "the most important thing" that happened to him at Wynyard (33), the first of the four boarding schools he would attend. Lewis became a student there in September 1908, when he was nine, and left in July 1910, when he was eleven. "There first I became an effective believer," Lewis writes.

The term *effective believer* suggests that at Wynyard Jack became more than a nominal Christian. He goes on to describe what this meant for him, writing, "I began seriously to pray and to read my Bible and to attempt to obey my conscience" (34). And in stating that he *began* these practices at Wynyard, Lewis tells us that he was not doing these things previously, at least not in a serious way. In the letter of February 15, 1946, mentioned earlier, he goes on to say, "I abandoned all belief in Christianity at about the age of fourteen" (*CLII*, 702). From these statements it would seem that as a young person Lewis had some Christian beliefs and attempted to live out those beliefs, but only after he left Little Lea and only for a while.

But again we are getting ahead of ourselves.

Although born and baptized as Clive, Lewis soon took a disliking to the name his parents had given him. Sometime around the age of four, he marched up to his mother and, pointing at himself, declared that he was now to be known as "Jacksie." This name, later shortened to Jacks and then to just Jack, became the only name he would answer to. In his book *Jack's Life*, Douglas Gresham, Lewis's stepson, provides the following background on why Lewis chose this name: "It was actually because of a small dog that he was fond of that he picked the name Jacksie, which was what the dog was called. It was run over (probably by a horse and cart as there were almost no cars in the time and place where he was a child), and Jack, as he later became known, just took the name for himself" (2).

Years later Lewis would begin *The Voyage of the Dawn Treader* with the famous line: "Once there was a boy called Eustace Clarence Scrubb, and he almost deserved it" (3). With the similar sounds in *Eustace* and *Lewis* and the shared initials C and S, readers might see this as the author's partially veiled critique of his own given name. As we will see later, Clive Staples Lewis and Eustace Clarence Scrubb shared other traits as well, ones that went beyond the names they were given.

By one count, that of Chip Duncan, who made the documentary *The Magic Never Ends*, there are only thirty-eight photographs of Lewis in the world. Most are in black and white, the only kind that existed for much of Lewis's lifetime. All the early ones were taken by a professional photographer at his studio or at Little Lea, since personal cameras were virtually nonexistent then. Given his celebrity which began in the 1940s—Lewis was featured on the cover of *Time* magazine on September 8, 1947—and continued to his death in 1963, it is surprising that there are no moving images. The more famous photos are readily available by doing an online search for "C. S. Lewis."

In the few photos we have of Lewis as an infant, we see an otherwise unremarkable, curly haired baby dressed in conventional baby clothes. But in one picture of him as a little boy, around the time he decided he was no longer to be called Clive, we see him standing alone dressed in a sailor suit, what must have been a normal outfit for a young boy at the time. But what is standing next to him is curious. Young Jacksie is holding the string to a toy donkey, and riding on the donkey is Father Christmas.

Did these two toys come together as a set, or did Lewis combine them—in the way that he would later combine divergent elements in Narnia? Was it Lewis who picked Father Christmas from all his toys to appear with him in the picture? Was the young Lewis already making up imaginary stories that featured Father Christmas as he played with the toy figure?

In his book *The Most Reluctant Convert*, David Downing suggests that the episode of Lewis choosing his own name is revealing. "This same boy," Downing writes, "who chose to define himself at the age of four, apart from the expectations and desires of those around him, would spend the rest of his life defining himself, and his world, differently from the conventions that he had inherited" (19). Whether writing fiction in a style the world had never seen, or deciding for himself—as an Oxford don and a layman—how public he should be about his Christian faith, or choosing late in life to marry an American divorcée, Lewis certainly would not hesitate to break from inherited conventions when he felt the need.

They Taught Me Longing

Good parents, good food, and a garden large enough to play in— this is how Lewis summarizes his early childhood in *Surprised by Joy*. He then lists two additional blessings from this time at Dundela Villas, before the move to the new house during his seventh year. The first blessing was the family's nurse, Lizzie Endicott, a working-class woman of local Irish stock who Lewis reports was as simply good as a human could be.

The other blessing was his brother.

"Though three years my senior, he never seemed to be an elder brother," Lewis writes (6). From the very start, he goes on to state, they were more than allies.

They were confederates.

If *Surprised by Joy* is the most important source of primary information we have about Lewis's early life, it could be argued that the second most important primary source is a lengthy essay written by Warren Lewis to appear at the front of *Letters of C. S. Lewis*, which was first published in 1966, two and a half years after Jack's death. This "Memoir of C. S. Lewis" opens with Warnie's comment that his earliest memories of his brother are of a "vociferous disturber" of the domestic peace and a "rival claimant" to their mother's attention (21). This initial stage quickly passed, and Warnie writes that during their childhood the brothers laid the foundations of an intimate friendship which became the greatest happiness of his life and lasted unbroken until Jack's death.

In the second paragraph, the memoir takes a curious turn. Looking back over his brother's life and all his accomplishments, Warnie notes, "I feel that one particular and even trivial circumstance in our early life together needs some emphasis" (21). What was this trivial element which played such a significant role in his younger brother's development? What could this circumstance be which Warnie claims has been overlooked and thus needs, as he says, greater emphasis? "I refer," he writes, "to the wetness of Irish weather, and the nervousness of the parents of that time about damp and exposure."

Warnie explains how the frequent Irish rain and the prevalent fear of exposure was such an influence.

> By the standards of present-day childhood in England, we spent an extraordinary amount of our time shut up indoors. We would gaze out of our nursery window at the slanting rain and the grey skies, and there, beyond a mile or so of sodden meadow, we would see the dim line of the Castlereagh Hills—our world's limit, a distant land, strange and unattainable. But we always had pencils, paper, chalk and paintboxes, and this recurring imprisonment gave us occasion and stimulus to develop the habit of creative imagination. . . . And so, in circumstance that might have been merely dull and depressing, my brother's gifts began to develop; and it may not be fanciful to see, in that childhood staring out to unattainable hills, some first beginnings of a vision and viewpoint that ran through the work of his maturity. (21)

In *Surprised by Joy*, Lewis says nothing about the rain but does mention the Castlereagh Hills the brothers could see from their window at the Dundela Villas house. "They were not very far off," he writes, "but they were, to children, quite unattainable" (7). He concludes with the observation, "They taught me longing."

And this was, Lewis notes, before he had turned six years old.

Besides this experience of longing evoked by the distant hills, Lewis records another defining experience in *Surprised by Joy* which took place during this period at the Dundela Villas house, an experience that modern readers both may and may not be able to relate to. One morning young Jack was playing inside and his brother came in, carrying the lid from a container for cookies—the lid of a biscuit tin, Lewis calls it. Warnie had covered the lid with moss and then added flowers and twigs to make it into sort of a garden in miniature.

What Warnie's beautiful, little toy garden did was to give Lewis a whole new view of the natural world. He describes the effect it had on him: "It made me aware of nature—not, indeed, as a storehouse of forms and colors but as something cool, dewy, fresh, exuberant" (7).

Lewis goes on to state that this impression became a lasting one that remained forever in his memory. Then he tells us that though he did not realize it until much later, this freshness and exuberance was for him a connection with the goodness of creation that still abides as a remnant and a reminder of an unfallen world. Lewis finishes his account of the incident with this statement: "As long as I live my imagination of Paradise will retain something of my brother's toy garden" (7).

Few people today have discovered Joy in a toy garden constructed in the lid of a biscuit tin, as Jack did, but they may have had an experience of the sacramental that can be found in nature, a fleeting sense of something wonderful, beyond what can be seen or touched.

Yet having a pleasant experience of nature is different from experiencing something in nature which points to something that transcends the natural world. Much later, in his *Reflections on the Psalms*, Lewis would explain the difference:

> To say that God created Nature, while it brings God and Nature into relation, also separates them. What makes and what is made must be two, not one. Thus the doctrine of Creation in one sense empties Nature of divinity. . . . But in another sense the same doctrine which empties Nature of her divinity also makes her an index, a symbol, a manifestation, of the Divine. . . . It is surely just because the natural objects are no longer taken to be themselves Divine that they can now be magnificent symbols of Divinity. . . . The doctrine of Creation leaves Nature full of manifestations which show the presence of God, and created energies which serve Him. (80–81)

In *Surprised by Joy*, Lewis makes a final observation about his experience with Warnie's toy garden: "That was the first beauty I ever knew" (7). Here in the early pages of his autography, he does not expand on the meaning of this beauty. Perhaps he does not analyze it because, at this point in his life, young Jacksie would not have thought much about what was behind this experience. But later in life, Lewis would have much to say about the beauty we find in nature—what its source is, what it points to, and why it moves us so deeply. He addresses all these topics perhaps nowhere as powerfully or as compellingly as in a passage from "The Weight of Glory." In it we can find Lewis's expression of the meaning behind his toy-garden experience.

> Our lifelong nostalgia, our longing to be reunited with something in the universe from which we now feel cut off . . . is not mere neurotic fantasy, but the truest index of our real situation. . . . We want . . . something the books on aesthetics take little notice of. . . . We do not want merely to see beauty. . . . We want something else which can hardly be put into words—to be united with the beauty we see, to pass into it, to receive it into ourselves, to bathe in it, to become part of it. (42)

In the very last chapter of the very last book he would write, *Letters to Malcolm*—which was published after his death—Lewis thinks back to his earliest memories, back to his first experience of beauty and how the memory of it had a lifelong effect on him. Borrowing a phrase from a poem by his friend Owen Barfield, Lewis writes, "The dullest of us knows how memory can transfigure; how often some momentary glimpse of beauty in boyhood is 'a whisper which memory will warehouse as a shout'" (122).

This whisper of beauty in Warnie's biscuit-lid garden would become a shout in Lewis's memory, an unforgettable pointer to something, or Someone, beyond nature.

Little Lea

In April 1905, Albert and Flora Lewis moved with their growing boys into a bigger house which reflected Albert's rising income and the Lewises' rising status in Belfast society. They named their new home—which Albert had specially though inexpertly built near the more open outskirts of town—Little Lea.

In *Surprised by Joy*, we are told that the move, made when Lewis was six, was the first great change in his life, so life-changing that Lewis maintains that the new house is almost a major character in his story. In his description of the effect that the rambling, three-story house had on him, we find one of the most quoted passages Lewis ever wrote: "I am the product of long corridors, empty sunlit rooms, upstairs indoor silences, attics explored in solitude, distant noises of gurgling cisterns and pipes, and the noise of wind under the tiles. Also of endless books" (10).

Often when this passage is cited, readers are immediately pointed to the "endless books" in Lewis's concluding element— books, as he describes, in the study, the drawing room, the cloakroom, and the bedroom; books two deep in the great bookcase; books piled on the landing and even higher in the attic. Certainly books featured prominently as vehicles of the Joy that Lewis would experience. But before turning to those books, we first need to pause and see those long corridors at Little Lea and look into those empty sunlit rooms. We need to go upstairs with young Jack and hear the indoor silences broken only by the faint gurgle of cisterns and pipes, and, especially, we need to stop and listen to the sound of the wind as it swooshes under the tiles. There was something about the mysterious, tranquil, eerie solitude in the new house that not only provided the setting for Lewis's deep longing but actually helped evoke it.

Without the move to Little Lea, there would still have been experiences of Joy in Lewis's early life, but perhaps they would not have been so strong nor have come so often.

In his autobiography, Lewis tells us that when he was young, Little Lea seemed to him more like a city than a house. We find Lewis's nod to his boyhood home in his description of the Professor's house in *The Lion, the Witch and the Wardrobe*. In chapter 1 the narrator tells us, "It was the sort of house that you never seem to come to the end of, and it was full of unexpected places" (6). The four Pevensies find that the house has many spare rooms, including one that is "quite empty except for one big wardrobe." The children also discover that—like Little Lea—the mysterious house has rooms and rooms lined with books.

All great writers began as great readers. And young Jack was no exception. Lewis tells us in his autobiography that he was allowed to read any book he wanted to from the seemingly endless supply at Little Lea. He points out that being able to find a new book was as easy and as certain as walking into a field and finding a new blade of grass. During the recurrent rainy afternoons, he read volume after volume, books that were suitable for a child and, as he tells us, books that were most emphatically not.

The young Lewis brothers claimed one of the many attic spaces explored in solitude to become their dayroom, a remote hideaway which under normal circumstances was off-limits to everyone else. They named it the "little end room." "There I kept my pen and inkpot," Lewis records in *Surprised by Joy*. "Here my first stories were written" (12–13).

In his "Memoir of C. S. Lewis," Warnie offers this description of Little Lea's mysterious nooks and crannies and the room they staked out for themselves:

> The new house itself was a child's delight, by reason of its atrociously uneconomical design: on the top floor, cupboard-like doors opened into huge, dark, wasted spaces under the roof, tunnel-like passages through which children could crawl from one space into another. . . . Best of all, we had our own dayroom in the attic. . . . In this glorious privacy, . . . our secret life flourished wonderfully. (23)

Years later Lewis would include a passage in *The Magician's Nephew*—a story set during the same time period when he and Warnie were boys at Little Lea—which calls to mind both the rainy days which kept the brothers indoors so often and the mysterious spaces they discovered under the roof of Little Lea. We are told that Digory and Polly's adventures began "chiefly because it was one of the wettest and coldest summers there had been for years" (8). Then Lewis's narrator explains:

> That drove them to do indoor things: you might say, indoor exploration. It is wonderful how much exploring you can do with a stump of a candle in a big house. . . . Polly had discovered long ago that if you opened a certain little door in the box-room attic of her house you would find the cistern and a dark place behind it which you could get into by a little careful climbing. . . . Polly had used the bit of the tunnel just beside the cistern as a smugglers' cave. . . . Here she kept a cash-box containing various treasures, and a story she was writing and usually a few apples.

One important benefit of the move to Little Lea had nothing to do with the house itself. Warnie reports in his memoir: "Our new house, 'Little Lea,' was on the borderline—suburb one way, open hilly farmland the other. We both had bicycles, and in these golden years before school, Jack developed a passionate and lifelong devotion to County Down" (23).

There is a famous picture, taken in 1908, of the two brothers standing on a country lane proudly holding their bikes. Later in life, fellow Ulsterman David Bleakley would record Lewis telling him, "Heaven is Oxford lifted and placed in the middle of County Down" (53). Lewis would later turn to the Irish countryside he explored as a child as his model for the landscape of Narnia, much as his friend J. R. R. Tolkien would base the Shire on memories of his boyhood home in rural Sarehole, England.

Soon after the move to Little Lea, Warnie, who had turned ten, was sent off to boarding school in England. Although his brother still came home for vacations and summers, Jack was now alone for much of the time. He was taught French and Latin by his mother, and all other subjects by his governess, Annie Harper. In his autobiography, Lewis tells us that he was an intolerable chatterbox at this time in his life, talking with his parents, his grandfather (who had moved in with them), the governess, the maids, and the gardener. Yet despite all these people that he could and did talk with, he also notes that his life was increasingly one of solitude, during which he would do two things: read stories and create his own, complete with illustrations.

Except for the surroundings, which are now quite built up, Little Lea stands today at 76 Circular Drive on Belfast's northeast side much as it did when it served as the Lewis family residence. The steps leading to the front entrance are still flanked by the low brick walls which can be clearly seen in the well-known Lewis family photo, and the walls are still topped with the same large decorative balls. In the photograph, Warnie is seen slouching against one of them, hands in his pockets. Unlike St. Mark's, which welcomes Lewis fans who make their way there from all over the world, Little Lea is privately owned and not open to the public. To tour the inside of a home Lewis lived in, visitors must travel to Headington, England, and the Kilns, the house he resided in for thirty-three years, from 1930 until his death.

Three Seminal Experiences of Joy—Like Prior Experiences or Something New?

Today when people try to read the personal narratives of famous Christian mystics from long ago—figures such as St. John of the Cross, Julian of Norwich, and Hildegard von Bingen—they sometimes find the accounts of their mystical experiences confusing and, at times, almost incomprehensible.

Lewis's account, too, can sometimes be a bit perplexing.

During the first few years after the move to Little Lea in 1905, Lewis again found himself surprised by the experience of Joy. He records three specific instances in his autobiography—and implies more went unrecorded. What is unclear is whether he saw these experiences at Little Lea as being of the same type as his early experiences of Warnie's toy garden and the distant Castlereagh Hills or as the beginning of something more profound. We can find evidence for both of these conclusions, but perhaps it does not really matter all that much.

Adding to the confusion is the fact that the first of these encounters of Joy after the move to Little Lea was actually, as Lewis explains in his autobiography, "the memory of a memory" (16). As Lewis writes *Surprised by Joy* in his fifties, he tells the story of a summer's day when he was standing by a flowering currant bush at Little Lea when he was six, seven, or eight, and suddenly something—perhaps the bush, perhaps something else—caused him to remember the experience of the toy garden in the biscuit tin back at Dundela Villas when he was four or five. Lewis comments that this memory from his family's old house seemed like it was coming not from just a few years before but from centuries earlier.

How does Lewis describe this desire, this experience of Joy which he felt standing by the currant bush as the memory of the toy-garden experience came over him? He first tells us, "Milton's 'enormous bliss' of Eden (giving the full, ancient meaning to 'enormous') comes somewhere near it" (16). In alluding to Milton's use of this phrase in book 5 of *Paradise Lost*, Lewis wants us to think of a bliss which transcends all conventional norms or measurements. He also tells us that this enormous bliss was *not* a longing for Warnie's biscuit lid filled with moss. But what it was a longing for, Lewis does not say.

Lewis concludes his account of the experience with such a bold claim that here we must turn to his own words: "Before I knew what I desired, the desire itself was gone, the whole glimpse withdrawn, the world turned commonplace again, or only stirred by a longing for the longing that had just ceased. It had taken only a moment of time; and in a certain sense everything else that had ever happened to me was insignificant in comparison" (16).

Does Lewis really mean that the extraordinary experience he took such care to describe earlier—the toy-garden incident—was truly insignificant in comparison to his *memory* of it by the currant bush years later? And not only that, but insignificant compared to *everything else that had ever happened to him*? Perhaps. Perhaps that is the only way to put into words how experiences like these feel. Many years later, in an essay titled "The Long Way Round," an American named Joy Davidman— who after a long journey became a Christian and, later, after a different kind of journey across the Atlantic, also became Mrs. Joy Lewis—made a similar claim in her account of a mysterious experience that changed her life: "All my defenses—the walls of arrogance and cocksureness and self-love behind which I hid from God—went down momentarily and God came in. . . . There was a Person with me in that room, directly present to my consciousness—a Person so real that all my previous life was by comparison a mere shadow play" (23).

In describing his unearthly experiences in chapter 1 of his autobiography, Lewis does not use the word God—not at this point. But note the similarities between the ways Lewis describes his three encounters and the account Joy Davidman gives in conclusion: "I myself was more alive than I had ever been; it was like waking from sleep. So intense a life cannot be endured long by flesh and blood; we must ordinarily take our life watered down, diluted as it were, by time and space and matter. My perception of God lasted perhaps half a minute" (23).

The second special experience of longing which Lewis tells us about in *Surprised by Joy* was prompted by the Beatrix Potter book *The Tale of Squirrel Nutkin*. "It troubled me," he writes, "with what I can only describe as the Idea of Autumn" (16). He points out that although he loved all the Potter books, he did not get this special feeling from any of the others—only *Squirrel Nutkin*. This Idea of Autumn, Lewis reports, was also an experience of intense desire, one that he admits came as a surprise and had the same sense of "incalculable importance" as his experience by the currant bush (17).

The Tale of Squirrel Nutkin was published in August 1903, three months before Jack's fifth birthday. Like Potter's first book, *The Tale of Peter Rabbit*, which had come out a year earlier in 1902, it was an instant success in England and Ireland. That said, readers of *Surprised by Joy* who search out *Squirrel Nutkin* because of its association with Lewis may be baffled as to why this book affected him so deeply. Besides telling us that it evoked the Idea of Autumn, Lewis does not elaborate on what it was in the book that affected him so. Perhaps it was the story's setting which moved him. Perhaps it was the illustrations—as he singles them out for a brief mention in chapter 3 of *An Experiment in Criticism* and also in the earlier manuscript version of *Surprised by Joy* (which Walter Hooper has titled "Early Prose Joy"). In *The Tale of Squirrel Nutkin*, we find this description which offers a glimpse of the season: "One autumn when the nuts were ripe, and the leaves on the hazel bushes were golden and green—Nutkin and Twinkle-berry and all the other little squirrels came out of the wood, and down to the edge of the lake" (6). Elsewhere we find fur-ther descriptions associated with autumn and the outdoors: a thin thread of smoke from a wood fire, yellow and scarlet oak apples, a crooked chestnut tree.

Whatever it was that evoked his experience of Joy, Lewis tells us that he returned to the book again and again, not to possess or gratify the desire, but to reawaken it.

This Idea of Autumn and its association with Joy never left Lewis. In a letter written to Arthur Greeves two decades later in October 1929, Lewis comments on a sense which he had more and more with each passing autumn and describes having, during a walk into Oxford, glimpses of "it"—the correspondents' name at the time for the poignant longing Lewis would later call Joy. He tells Arthur:

> Today I worked in the morning and afternoon and walked into town. . . . The real autumn tang in the air had begun. There was one of those almost white skies with a touch of frosty red over the town, and the beginnings of lovely coloring in the college's garden. I love the big kitchen garden there. There is something very attractive about rows of pots—and an old man potting— and greenhouses and celery trenches. . . . I saw both a squirrel and a fat old rat in Addison's walk, and had glimpses of "it."
>
> I think almost more every year in autumn I get the sense, just as the mere nature and voluptuous life of the world is dying, of something else coming awake. You know the feeling, of course, as well as I do. I wonder is it significant—in stories nymphs slip out of the tree just as the ordinary life of the wood is settling down for the night. Does the death of the natural always mean the birth of the spiritual? (*CLI*, 831–32)

Readers who may not be moved by *The Tale of Squirrel Nutkin* may have been moved by a crisp, clear autumn day—moved in a way that went beyond the merely physical qualities that were present. Lewis remained a Beatrix Potter fan all his life. In a letter dated November 30, 1942, he writes of her "secure place among the masters of English prose" and confesses that he and

Tolkien had often toyed with the idea of making a pilgrimage to visit her (*CLII*, 538).

The third of these seminal experiences of Joy at Little Lea came to Lewis through lines found in a long work by the American poet Henry Wadsworth Longfellow titled *The Saga of King Olaf*. Just as before, when Lewis noted that he was not deeply affected by any other Beatrix Potter books, only *Squirrel Nutkin*, here again he records in *Surprised by Joy* that he was fond of the work only in a causal or shallow way, for its story and strong rhythmic verse. But then he tells us that when he turned a page and came across the opening lines from Longfellow's translation of "Tegner's Drapa," he was suddenly lifted up into "huge regions of northern sky" (17). These are the lines Lewis read:

> I heard a voice that cried,
> Balder the beautiful
> Is dead, is dead—

What it was about these lines and no others that moved him, Lewis does not say, and perhaps did not know. He confesses that as a young boy reading the poem, he knew nothing about Balder. It is safe to say that not many Lewis fans will be moved in the same way that Lewis was by these lines, but a few years later Lewis would become friends with a neighbor named Arthur Greeves, mentioned earlier, who shared his passion for Norse legends. Seven chapters later in *Surprised by Joy*, Lewis describes their common response to H. A. Guerber's *Myths of the Norsemen*, as he and Greeves discovered that they both "knew the stab of Joy and that, for both, the arrow was shot from the North" (130).

If readers today find it hard to relate to Lewis's account of being transported to huge regions of northern sky by Longfellow's lament for Balder, they may be moved, and moved quite deeply, by the mysterious longing found in Lewis's own story

The Horse and His Boy. In this Chronicle of Narnia, published in 1954, Lewis tells about a young boy named Shasta who is inexplicably interested in everything that lies to the North and often finds himself eagerly looking to the North, until one day he meets a talking horse named Bree.

"I've been longing to go to the North all my life," Shasta tells him in a secret conversation (14).

"Of course you have," Bree responds, for to the North lies Narnia, the land where Shasta belongs, his real country.

"Narnia and the North!" becomes their rallying cry, a phrase that may transport today's readers in perhaps much the same ways as "Balder the beautiful is dead" transported young Jack as he sat reading in the little end room of Little Lea.

It is after describing these three mysterious and fleeting experiences of Joy at Little Lea—the memory of Warnie's toy garden while standing at a currant bush, the Idea of Autumn evoked by *The Tale of Squirrel Nutkin*, and the uplift into huge regions of northern sky brought on through lines by Longfellow—that Lewis makes the statement, "The central story of my life is about nothing else." George Sayer, who was first Lewis's student, then later his close friend and biographer, suggests that these episodes were mystical experiences of the presence of God and notes how they arose from such "seemingly incongruous events" (52). Then Sayer points out, "Incongruous, that is, until one remembers that the Spirit 'blows where it listeth.'"

We could say that the Spirit blew not only *where* and *when* it desired in Lewis's youth but also *how* it willed to—in his case, *not* through the Sunday school lessons and stained-glass images at St. Mark's, as might have been expected. As we will learn, what later would link all of Lewis's incongruous surprises of Joy was what—or Who—was behind them.

Taking a different tack, we could say that Lewis's experiences of Joy were also linked by a certain kind of receptivity in the young Jack, an openness that stayed with him all his life. Biographer Alan Jacobs suggests that Lewis's most significant defining characteristic was his willingness to be enchanted—a profound openness to delight joined with the sense that there is "more to the world than meets the jaundiced eye" (xxi). Jacobs makes the case that later in life Lewis's work would be connected by a desire to reverse or undo the "disenchantment of the world" (188), to break the powerful spell that causes us to see the physical world as nothing more than a meaningless mass of molecules and atoms—to think that a star is just a ball of gas or that a flowering currant bush is just a bunch of petals, leaves, and branches.

Much later, in *Letters to Malcolm*, Lewis would write that special holy places should serve to remind us that "every bush (could we but perceive it) is a Burning Bush" (75), a reference to not only the burning bush that Moses saw but perhaps also to the currant bush at Little Lea. Lewis then offers a moving proposition: "We may ignore, but we can nowhere evade, the presence of God. The world is crowded with Him. He walks everywhere incognito. And the incognito is not always hard to penetrate." So what is our role? What need we do to be surprised by Joy? Lewis describes our task this way: "The real labor is to remember, to attend. In fact, to come awake. Still more, to remain awake."

The answer we see modeled in Lewis's life is that we must remain receptive.

As Lewis shifts from describing these three seminal experiences of Joy to his next major focus in his autobiography, the death of his mother, he makes a statement intended to serve as a transition but which is interesting for something it tells us. He writes, "I cannot be absolutely sure whether the things I have just been speaking of happened before or after the great loss which befell our family and to which I must now turn" (18). The death of Flora Lewis when Jack was only nine, a staggering blow that will be examined in the next chapter, would mark the end of his childhood and the start of his boyhood. When he tells us that these encounters might have happened after or before her death, Lewis makes it clear that not even the life or the death of his mother could separate him from these stabs of Joy.

Schoolboy and Adolescent

(1 9 0 8 – 1 9 1 3)

This is a story about something that happened long ago
when your grandfather was a child. . . . In those days,
if you were a boy you had to wear a stiff Eton Collar
every day, and schools were usually nastier than now.

—*The Magician's Nephew*, chapter 1

The End of Childhood and the Old Security

In addition to the epigraph found at the beginning of his autobiography, "Surprised by Joy—impatient as the wind," Lewis
also includes an epigraph at the start of each chapter. Chapter
1, "The First Years," opens with words from Milton's *Paradise
Lost*: "Happy, but for so happy ill secured."

The reason Lewis selected this line is made plain in the chapter's final pages.

In book 4 of *Paradise Lost*, Satan looks in on the Garden of Eden and comments on the fragile happiness of Adam and Eve. The line Lewis quotes is in italics:

> Ah! gentle pair, ye little think how nigh
> Your change approaches, when all these delights
> Will vanish, and deliver ye to woe;
> More woe, the more your taste is now of joy;
> *Happy, but for so happy ill secured*
> Long to continue, and this high seat, your Heaven,
> Ill fenced for Heaven to keep out such a foe
> As now is entered (4:366–73)

Surely the blissful world of Lewis's childhood was "ill fenced" against tragedy, for it was only a matter of time until pain and loss would invade it. Later, in *The Problem of Pain*, Lewis would take as one of his main premises that all of us, young and old, are ill-secured for happiness to continue for very long in this world—at least in its normal, everyday sense.

Through his use of this epigraph—"Happy, but for so happy ill secured"—Lewis wants readers to picture the two brothers, in some sense, like the innocent Adam and Eve, a gentle pair living in an idyllic world. He does *not* want us to extend the comparison with Adam and Eve and to see the boys' expulsion from their Eden as something they themselves were responsible for.

That said, the young Lewis must have felt as though his paradise had truly been lost.

In 1907 Flora began to display a number of symptoms—among them tiredness, a loss of appetite, and worsening abdominal pains. Early the following year, several doctors were called to the house for a consultation—one that would result in a dreadful diagnosis. In *Surprised by Joy*, Lewis begins the account of their visit to Little Lea with these words: "There came a night when I was ill and crying both with headache and toothache and distressed because my mother did not come to me. That was because she was ill too" (18). He remembers several doctors being present, many comings and goings, doors shutting and opening, and many voices, before his father finally arrived at his room in tears with the bad news of the diagnosis: Jack's mother had cancer.

An operation was urgently advised, and Flora underwent surgery for abdominal cancer on February 15, 1908. As was normal in those days, it took place in the home. In twelve short words, Lewis records what happened next. There followed "an apparent convalescence, a return of the disease, increasing pain, and death" (18).

Flora passed away at home six months following her surgery, on the morning of August 23, 1908. She was forty-six. Her older son, Warnie, was thirteen. Jack was nine.

Flora's gradual decline had put a strain on Albert, whose nerves had never been very steady. In fact, her death was a loss that Lewis claims his father never fully recovered from, forcing Jack and Warnie to turn to each other for comfort. In *Surprised by Joy*, Lewis describes himself and Warnie at this time as "two frightened urchins huddled for warmth in a bleak world" (19).

In the opening sentence of the preface, Lewis tells us that he has two purposes in *Surprised by Joy*. His goal was to tell how he passed from atheism to Christianity and "to correct one or two false notions that seem to have got about" (vii). We get the sense that by the time he was writing his autobiography in the late 1940s and early 1950s, there had been speculation about how his mother's death affected his religious beliefs and that Lewis wanted to set the record straight, for at the end of chapter 1 he writes, "My mother's death was the occasion of what some (but not I) might regard as my first religious experience" (20).

One reason people may have regarded Lewis's loss of his mother as a religious experience was that when she was declared critically ill with cancer, young Jack prayed fervently for her to recover. After her death, he continued his prayers, but now his request was that she would miraculously return to life. Here we must turn to Lewis's own account in *Surprised by Joy*:

> When her case was pronounced hopeless I remembered what I had been taught; that prayers offered in faith would be granted. I accordingly set myself to produce by will power a firm belief that my prayers for her recovery would be successful; and, as I thought, I achieved it. When nevertheless she died I shifted my ground and worked myself into a belief that there was to be a miracle. (20)

Lewis explains that when he was nine, he approached God, or rather his idea of God, with neither love, nor awe, nor fear. At this time he did not view God as Savior or even as Judge but merely as a sort of Magician, an entity who, if requested in the proper way—something Lewis tried very hard to do—would grant whatever was requested of him. The young Lewis expected this genie-like Magician, after having granted the petitioner's wish, to then go back into his bottle until needed again, allowing life to go on as usual. Lewis points out that "faith" of this sort—and he puts the word in quotation marks to indicate he does not mean genuine faith here—must often be generated by children (21).

Lewis concludes that whether the desired goal of this childish, inauthentic faith is achieved is of no religious importance, and he classifies his prayers at this time as being irreligious. In *Planets in Peril*, David Downing sums up young Jack's lack of a religious experience at the time of Flora's death this way: "The failure of his prayers did not produce a loss of belief in him because there was no genuine belief there in the first place" (27).

Much later, in *Letters to Malcolm*, Lewis would write of the danger of seeing God as a divine vending machine and prayer merely as an attempt to "pull the right wires" (15).

If, as Lewis claims, his mother's death had no religious effect on him, might the loss of his beloved mother—who had also been his teacher and the parent he was most attached to—have affected Lewis's later development as a writer of a certain kind of fantasy literature?

Any speculation would be purely conjecture and precisely the sort of psychoanalyzing about authors which Lewis detested. Still, a set of coincidences which can at least be labeled remarkable confronts us. Flora Lewis died in August 1908, when Clive Staples was just short of his tenth birthday. Mabel Tolkien died in November 1904, when her son John Ronald Reuel was twelve. Helen MacDonald died in 1832, when her son George was eight years old. Three of the greatest fantasy writers in the English language each suffered the childhood loss of his mother, devastating tragedies that may have helped spur their interest in imaginative realms of their own creation.

Lewis ends chapter 1 of *Surprised by Joy* with what has become one of its most poignant and well-known passages: "With my mother's death all settled happiness, all that was tranquil and reliable, disappeared from my life. There was to be much fun, many pleasures, many stabs of Joy; but no more of the old security. It was sea and islands now; the great continent had sunk like Atlantis" (21).

Lewis's Fictional Depictions of Death

There is an old adage that writers should write about what they know. Certainly by the time Lewis was in his thirties and forties and began writing the works he would become famous for, one thing he was well acquainted with was death, through the loss of both his mother and his father, and also the death of other relatives, neighbors, and many of the men he served with in World War I. In Lewis's fiction we find a number of depictions of death. What stands out when we compare them to the "sea and islands" passage from *Surprised by Joy* is their radically different tone. Lewis the middle-aged, Christian author had a very different perspective on death from young Jack, the grief-stricken nine-year-old.

Most accounts of Flora's death and Jack's struggle to come to terms with it also point to Lewis's story of the young Digory Kirke and his desire to save his ailing mother in *The Magician's Nephew*. In the opening pages, Digory is introduced to us as a boy who is "so miserable that he didn't care who knew he had been crying" (4). He tells Polly Plummer, who is to become his close friend and fellow traveler to Narnia, that if she had his troubles, she would cry too. He recounts a long list of woes, ending with the worst: "And if your Mother was ill and was going to—going to—die" (6).

In the end, Lewis gives the fictional mother and son the happy ending his own childhood lacked. After having been faithful in all his tasks in Narnia, Digory receives an apple to take back home which restores his mother to health. Through the adventure, Lewis has Digory learn several important lessons which he himself learned only as an adult after his conversion. Initially Digory thinks about trying to strike some kind of deal with Aslan in exchange for his mother's health, but he quickly realizes that Aslan is "not at all the sort of person one could try to make bargains with" (153).

Finally, with a lump in his throat and tears in his eyes, Digory blurts out a plea that is almost a prayer: "But please, please—won't you—can't you give me something that will cure Mother?" (154). Digory then looks up at Aslan, and we are told that what Digory sees then surprises him "as much as anything in his whole life." Digory discovers that Aslan's eyes are also filled with tears, tears even bigger than his own, and he realizes that the lion "must really be sorrier about his Mother than he was himself."

Another lesson Lewis has Digory learn in *The Magician's Nephew*, yet a third thing which young Jack Lewis did not see in 1908, is that "there might be things more terrible even than losing someone you love by death" (191). In fact, when the adult Lewis depicts actual death in his fiction—technically Digory's mother is near death—he looks at death which has lost its sting.

In *Surprised by Joy*, Lewis tells us that the grief he felt at his mother's death was further compounded by the horror he suffered upon being shown her lifeless body. Lewis recalls: "I was taken into the bedroom where my mother lay dead; as they say, 'to see her,' in reality, as I at once knew, 'to see it.' There was nothing that a grown-up would call disfigurement—except for that total disfigurement which is death itself. Grief was overwhelmed in terror" (20).

Four decades later, Lewis would create a very different kind of encounter at the end of *The Silver Chair*, when the young Eustace Scrubb views the dead body of Caspian, who in life had been his friend. In the final chapter, fittingly titled "The Healing of Harms," Eustace and Jill find themselves in Aslan's country alongside a stream where Caspian's corpse—described as wrinkled and pale and having sunken cheeks—can be seen beneath the flowing water. For a time, the two children and Aslan simply stand together and weep. Then Aslan commands Eustace to pluck a thorn and drive it into his paw. A great drop of red blood splashes into the stream over the lifeless body. Then readers are told:

> The dead King began to be changed. His white beard turned to gray, and from gray to yellow, and got shorter and vanished

altogether; and his sunken cheeks grew round and fresh, and
the wrinkles were smoothed, and his eyes opened, and his eyes
and lips both laughed, and suddenly he leaped up and stood
before them—a very young man or a boy. (But Jill couldn't say
which, because of people having no particular ages in Aslan's
country. . . .) And he rushed to Aslan and flung his arms as far
as they would go round the huge neck; and he gave Aslan the
strong kisses of a King, and Aslan gave him the wild kisses of
a Lion. (238–39)

If, at Flora's death, grief was overwhelmed by the terror of
her lifeless body, at Caspian's death and resurrection Lewis has
grief overwhelmed by happiness.

Lewis provides several other depictions of death and life
after death in his fiction. Notable among them is his portrait
of the "Bright People" of heaven we find in *The Great Divorce*.
But perhaps nowhere does Lewis offer a more uplifting repre-
sentation of the end of this life than in the final pages of *The
Screwtape Letters*. In this work, published in 1942, a senior devil
named Screwtape offers advice to his nephew, a junior tempter
named Wormwood, on the best way to lead his "patient" to
hell. In the end all their plans fail, as the man is killed by an air
raid while in a state of grace. In the final letter Lewis, through
Screwtape, imagines what Christian death might be like—and
in this description we can find aspects of Flora's death now
transformed.

Just think . . . what he felt at that moment; as if a scab had
fallen from an old sore, . . . as if he shuffled off for good and all
a defiled, wet, clinging garment. . . . He got through so easily!
No gradual misgivings, no doctor's sentence, no nursing home,
no operating theatre, no false hopes of life; sheer instantaneous
liberation. One moment it seemed to be all our world; . . . next
moment all this was gone, gone like a bad dream, never again
to be of any account. (172)

In an earlier letter from Screwtape, readers learned that the patient's girlfriend and mother were praying that he be kept safe and not die—much as Jack prayed for his mother. Screwtape explained that humans had been taught by their tempters "to regard death as the prime evil and survival as the greatest good" (154). If Lewis had this perspective as a boy experiencing his mother's death, he later came to see death in a very different light.

Near the very end of *Letters to an American Lady*, in a letter from June 1963, just five months before Lewis's own death, he offers these words to Mary Willis Shelburne, who was old and frail and knew that the end of this life was not far off:

> Can you not see death as the friend and deliverer? It means stripping off that body which is tormenting you: like taking off a hairshirt or getting out of a dungeon. What is there to be afraid of? You have long attempted (and none of us does more) a Christian life. Your sins are confessed and absolved. Has this world been so kind to you that you should leave it with regret? There are better things ahead than any we leave behind. (117)

There are better things ahead than any we leave behind. This would be Lewis's position near the end of his own life. As a young boy, he found nothing about death comforting.

As we saw, in the final sentences from chapter 1 of *Surprised by Joy*, Lewis reports the loss of "the old security." The "great continent" was gone. Life after his mother's death was only "sea and islands." Now, at the start of chapter 2, Lewis returns to this thought: "All security seemed to be taken from me; there was no solid ground beneath my feet" (39).

In *Perelandra*, published in 1943 as the second book in Lewis's Space Trilogy, we find an interesting complement to these passages. Its protagonist, a philologist named Elwin Ransom, travels to the planet Venus. There he meets an Eve figure, referred to as the Green Lady, who has been forbidden not from eating a certain fruit but from staying the night on the Fixed Land. Though she may visit the stable continent during the day, Maleldil has commanded that she must return each night to one of the planet's floating islands. In the final chapter, the Green Lady comes to understand the reason for her initial restriction to a life of sea and islands, as she tells Ransom:

> The reason for not yet living on the Fixed Land is now so plain. How could I wish to live there except because it was Fixed? And why should I desire the Fixed except to make sure—to be able on one day to command where I should be the next and what should happen to me? It was to reject the wave—to draw my hands out of Maleldil's, to say to Him, "Not thus, but thus"—to put in our own power what times should roll towards us. . . . That would have been cold love and feeble trust. (179)

Years after losing the fixed land that his mother had provided, years after he tried to say to God the Magician, "Not thus, but thus," Lewis would find a different kind of security. This security would not be the kind that put it in his power to command what should happen to him but the kind that required trust. Years after his mother's death, Lewis would find a way to live with confidence in a world of sea and islands.

Six Years and One Day

In the opening paragraph of *The Magician's Nephew*, a story Lewis set during the time when he was a schoolboy himself, the narrator tells us, "In those days, if you were a boy you had to wear a stiff Eton collar every day, and schools were usually nastier than now" (3). This is just one of many critical observations about the British educational system we find in the Chronicles of Narnia, comments that were based on Lewis's own dreadful experiences at school.

In the final chapter of *The Last Battle*, Peter, Susan, Edmund, and Lucy learn that they have come home to their real country and will never have to leave again. "There *was* a real railway accident," the lion tells them. "Your father and mother and all of you are—as you used to call it in the Shadowlands—dead" (210). Lewis then wants to express the very best news that could ever be expressed and thus, as he so frequently does, looks for the perfect metaphor to convey the profound feelings associated with this news. "The term is over," Lewis has Aslan explain. "The holidays have begun."

Negative statements about schools and education are so common in the Chronicles—one of the tasks Lewis assigns the children during their reign in *The Lion, the Witch and the Wardrobe* is to liberate young dwarfs and young satyrs from being sent to school—that readers have to look hard to find a positive one. In the relationship of the young Prince Caspian with his tutor, Doctor Cornelius, we see one of the rare depictions of the learning process as something to enjoy, not something to dread. As we will see later, their relationship has roots in Lewis's own story as well.

On September 18, 1908, just twenty-six days after his mother's death, young Jack Lewis was sent across the Irish Sea to Wynyard boarding school in Watford, England. He was two months shy of ten years old.

Six years and one day later, on September 19, 1914, Jack would get off the train at Great Bookham in Surrey, England, to begin three wonderful years of tutoring under William Kirkpatrick.

Though not without some bright spots, the six years he spent at the series of schools that came in between being tutored at home by his mother and governess and being tutored by Kirkpatrick were—even more so than his time at the front in World

War I—the bleakest years in Lewis's life. In a letter he wrote on March 24, 1962, one published in the collection *Letters to Children*, Lewis tells a young fan: "I was at three schools (all boarding schools) of which two were very horrid. I never hated anything so much, not even the front line trenches in World War I. Indeed the story is far *too* horrid to tell anyone of your age" (102).

Lewis simplifies his school history a bit here, for if we count the month he spent at Campbell in Belfast, he attended *four* schools: Wynyard (September 1908–July 1910), Campbell (September–November 1910), Cherbourg (January 1911–July 1913), and Malvern (September 1913–July 1914). While he did not really like any of the four institutions he was sent to, the two schools he found "very horrid" were the first and last ones he attended: Wynyard and Malvern.

A close look at the contents page of *Surprised by Joy* reveals a curious fact: Lewis devotes chapters 2 through 8—nearly half of the book's fifteen chapters—to these six years between 1908 and 1914. On page 22 young Jack leaves for the first time to travel to Wynyard and does not arrive in Great Bookham to meet his new tutor until page 132.

Why such a disproportionate ratio? Why does Lewis allocate 110 of the 238 pages—virtually half—of an autobiography covering the first thirty-three years of his life to a period of just six years?

Lewis tells us the answer, in part, right at the start, when he explains in the preface that *Surprised by Joy* is not intended to be a general autobiography but the story of his conversion. It will be Lewis's plan to include far more details from his early years. He explains his strategy this way:

> In the earlier chapters the net has to be spread pretty wide in order that, when the explicitly spiritual crisis arrives, the reader may understand what sort of person my childhood and adolescence

had made me. When the "build-up" is complete, I confine myself strictly to business and omit everything (however important by ordinary biographical standards) which seems, at that stage, irrelevant. (vii–viii)

If, as Lewis tells us, later in life he arrived at a spiritual crisis, these seven chapters on his school days help us to understand the origins of this crisis. In chapters 2 through 8, Lewis tells the story of a young person who got on a wrong track, how he made this wrong turn, and what led him to become so in need of a savior.

The Concentration Camp

Earlier it was claimed that Lewis's habit of writing with a nib pen was more like that of a medieval monk than today's methods. In that same vein, it could be argued that Wynyard School—located in Watford, England, eighteen miles northwest of London—was more like a dreadful school from a Dickens novel than a school today. If Lewis summarized his first years of childhood at Dundela Villas as good parents, good food, and a garden large enough to play in, his two years at Wynyard could be summarized as bad headmaster, bad food, no garden, and very little learning.

Sending a nine-year-old—accompanied only by his thirteen-year-old brother—to travel overnight on a steamship from Belfast to Fleetwood, England, and then by rail to Euston Station in London to connect to Watford, seems at least questionable by today's standards. But Lewis makes it clear that the journey was enjoyable and not out of the ordinary for boys to do on their own in those days. Flora had taken Warnie on his very first trip to boarding school in England in 1905, but afterward he traveled by himself. Beginning in 1908, he and Jack traveled by themselves, making the journey six times each year at the beginning and end of each of England's three trimesters. Scholar Richard James has estimated that by the time Lewis was eighteen and ready to enter Oxford, he would have made at least fifty-two of these trips coming or going across the Irish Sea (64).

In his autobiography, Lewis recounts how from the very start he was an excellent sailor and enjoyed traveling by ship—the reflection of the lights on the water, the warm smell of the engines, the rattle of the winches, and the taste of the salt spray on his lips. It was not the trip that was the hardship for young Jack, nor was it that he was going to boarding school at such a young age—something else that was not uncommon for the time and a practice generally considered to be good for young boys. The hardship was what awaited him at the school his father had chosen.

While undoubtedly many young boys have complained that their school was a concentration camp and the headmaster a lunatic, in Jack's case it was actually true. Like Wackford Squeers, the fictional headmaster in *Nicholas Nickleby*, Robert Capron, the real-life headmaster of Wynyard, took enjoyment in tyrannizing his pupils through frequent canings. Like Squeers, Capron—whom the boys referred to as Oldie—was viciously brutal, sometimes running the length of the schoolroom to build up force for one of his drubbings, as he called them, which he very regularly administered, often for little or no reason.

Chapter 2 of *Surprised by Joy* is titled "Concentration Camp," and Lewis assigns Wynyard the pseudonym "Belsen," after the Nazi prison camp. The epigraph he uses, "Arithmetic with Colored Rods," comes from an article Lewis had seen in the *Times Educational Supplement* in 1954, about the time he was finishing his autobiography. The article described an innovative and presumably fun practice of teaching arithmetic through the use of brightly colored rods with numbers on them. Lewis turns the phrase to refer to the endless sums the boys at Wynyard were forced to do every day—which was about all they did when it came to academics—and the drubbings they received from Oldie's rods for incorrect answers.

Already in decline and down to only eight boarders when the Lewis brothers attended, Wynyard was closed in 1910—a fortunate occurrence for Jack, as it forced Albert to send him to a new school after only two years (rather than the four Warnie had to endure). Shortly after the school's demise, Capron was declared insane and sent to an asylum.

I Became an Effective Believer

About two-thirds of the way through chapter 2 of *Surprised by Joy*, after telling us about Wynyard's horrid classes, horrid living conditions, and horrid headmaster, Lewis announces, "But I have not yet mentioned the most important thing that befell me at Oldie's" (33). One benefit came out of Lewis's time at the concentration camp, one that had little to do with the school itself. Twice every Sunday during the two years the young Lewis was at Wynyard, he and the other pupils were taken to St. John's Church in Watford. And there, Lewis writes, "I heard the doctrines of Christianity (as distinct from general 'uplift') taught by men who obviously believed them."

Is Lewis saying that he had not heard these doctrines at St. Mark's or that they were not believed in the obvious way they were at St. John's? Perhaps. In his account of how he came to faith at Wynyard, Lewis goes on to record that he and his school friends soon began to discuss religion often together in a way that was "entirely healthy and profitable . . . , with great gravity and without hysteria" (34), perhaps implying that in previous discussions back in Belfast religion was *not* discussed profitably but with hysteria.

And is Lewis saying here that his previous religious training consisted only of general uplift? Again, perhaps. In his memoir, Warnie comments that they were offered only the "dry husks of religion" during the "semi-political" churchgoing of their childhood (39).

Alternatively, perhaps Lewis simply was not old enough to hear the doctrines of Christianity until he got to Wynyard. Or perhaps during his pleasant childhood at Little Lea, Jack simply was not open to hearing them. Perhaps the hardships at Wynyard opened him to them. In *Surprised by Joy*, Lewis tells us what he got from St. John's but does not say much about what he did not get at St. Mark's. He simply states, "The effect was to bring to life what I would already have said that I believed" (33). So something good did come from Oldie's miserable school: "There first I became an effective believer."

What were these first steps of real faith like? What was Lewis's response to hearing Christian doctrines taught at St. John's by men who really believed them? Lewis records, "In this experience there was a great deal of fear" (33–34). He recalls certain moonlit nights as he lay awake in the curtain-less dormitory at Oldie's, the eerie silence broken only by the sound of the other boys' breathing, and states, "I feared for my soul" (34).

Some Christians might be skeptical or even critical of a faith that had a foundation not just of fear but, as we are told, "a great deal of fear." Not Lewis. He goes on to maintain, "The effect, so far as I can judge, was entirely good" (34). While, as we will see, Lewis understands that sometimes fear can be detrimental and there is a limit to how far it can grow a person's faith, about his religious fear at this time he insists, "I do not think there was more than was wholesome or even necessary."

In what sense could Lewis have found his fear wholesome and necessary? Here in chapter 2 of *Surprised by Joy*, he describes three positive effects this fear produced: he began to pray, to read his Bible, and to obey his conscience.

If we look to his other works, we find Lewis has more to say on the positive role of fear in the *initial* steps of faith. In chapter 6 of *The Problem of Pain*, Lewis points out:

> It is hardly complimentary to God that we should choose Him as an alternative to Hell: yet even this He accepts. The creature's illusion of self-sufficiency must, for the creature's sake, be shattered; and by trouble or fear of trouble on earth, by crude fear of the eternal flames, God shatters it "unmindful of His glory's diminution." (87)

It is notable that among the passages Lewis selected for *George MacDonald: An Anthology*, we find this one, which he titled "Fear": "Until a man has love, it is well he should have fear. So long as there are wild beasts about, it is better to be afraid than secure" (142). Lewis came across this passage in MacDonald's book *What's Mine's Mine*, where in a preceding sentence MacDonald uses an adjective to describe fear that Lewis would later borrow. MacDonald states, "Fear is a wholesome element in the human economy; they are merely silly who would banish it from all association with religion" (113).

I do not think there was more than was wholesome or even necessary.

In a letter dated December 8, 1941, Lewis tells his correspondent, "Fear isn't repentance—but it's all right as a *beginning*—much better at that stage than *not* being afraid" (*CLII*, 500).

In his autobiography, Lewis makes it clear that his own fear at this time was a start, a first step on his spiritual journey—not a final step. He concludes his discussion of these initial attempts at genuine faith by stating, "How I went back from *this beginning* you shall hear later" (34, emphasis added).

In chapter 1 we saw how when Lewis made his request to God that his mother recover, he did so "without love, without awe, even without fear" and viewed God at that time "neither as Savior nor as Judge" (21). Now at St. John's, Lewis came to see God not as Magician but as Judge and to approach him with fear. As Lewis comments, he would later go back from this beginning—to a complete loss of faith—before going forward to approach God with love and to finally see him as Savior.

Before leaving Lewis's first steps toward real belief at Wynyard, it should be noted that there is a kind of biography that claims to understand Lewis's life better than Lewis himself did. When Lewis claims that the fear he felt during this time was no more than was wholesome and even necessary and had an effect that was entirely good, there is a kind of biography that knows better.

For example, when Lewis tells us that at St. John's he heard the doctrines of Christianity, biographer Michael White leaves out Lewis's own description and instead tells us that the sermons Lewis heard were "largely meaningless" (26). White asserts that these meaningless sermons "succeeded in their purpose, terrifying the boy into acquiescence." White does not mention that Lewis himself says nothing about being terrified into acquiescence but instead claims to have become an "effective believer." When Lewis tells us that what really mattered was hearing "the doctrines of Christianity . . . taught by men who obviously believed them," White asserts that Lewis began to read his Bible at this time "thanks to the power of ritual and fear."

There is a kind of biography that looks at what Lewis tells us in his autobiography and, following the biographer's own set of presuppositions, claims to understand Lewis's life in ways that Lewis himself could not.

This is not that kind of biography.

Joy's Absence and Two Types of Books

What about the experience of Joy during the two years at Oldie's? Lewis simply tells us there was none.

In chapter 2 of his autobiography, he reports, "For many years Joy (as I have defined it) was not only absent but forgotten" (34). Readers already know that this hiatus will be temporary, for at the moving conclusion of chapter 1, Lewis explained that after his mother's death there would still be many stabs of Joy. But after telling us here that Joy was not only absent but forgotten, Lewis does not mention experiencing Joy again until almost forty pages later, in chapter 5, where it will return with his discovery of *Siegfried and the Twilight of the Gods*.

Why were these stabs of Joy absent, beginning at Wynyard and continuing, as Lewis says, for many years? Lewis gives us a partial answer, but here we must look at his statement in the context of his life at Wynyard, about which he writes:

> There was also a great decline in my imaginative life. For many years Joy (as I have defined it) was not only absent but forgotten. My reading was now mainly rubbish. . . . I read twaddling school stories in *The Captain*. The pleasure here was, in the proper sense, mere wish fulfillment . . . ; one enjoyed vicariously the triumphs of the hero. When the boy passes from nursery literature to school stories he is going down, not up. . . . The story of the unpromising boy who became captain of the First Eleven exists precisely to feed his real ambitions. (34–35)

Earlier, in comparing the surprise of Joy to the wind, Lewis suggested that its appearance was not something he could control—like the wind, it came or did not come as it willed. But in this passage, Lewis implies that there was something he could do to *hinder* the coming of Joy or to *foster* it—and it had to do with the kind of book he read. Lewis associates his lack of experience of Joy with the type of reading he was doing, though exactly how reading and Joy are interconnected he does not explain.

In his famous essay "On Three Ways of Writing for Children," Lewis asks us to lay two types of books side by side for comparison. The first type he calls a Boy's Book or a Girl's Book—another name for the "twaddling school stories" he began reading at Oldie's. Here, Lewis comments, we find the "immensely popular and successful schoolboy or schoolgirl" who "discovers the spy's plot or rides the horse that none of the cowboys can manage" (38). Lewis explains the appeal of the school story this way—and here we can find echoes of his statement about his reading at Wynyard.

> Its fulfillment on the level of imagination is in very truth compensatory: we run to it from the disappointments and humiliations of the real world: it sends us back to the real world undivinely discontented. For it is all flattery to the ego. The pleasure consists in picturing oneself the object of admiration.

Next in the essay, Lewis switches from the school story to the fairy tale—and in this broad category we might want to include stories like *The Tale of Squirrel Nutkin*, which inspired Lewis with the Idea of Autumn, and Longfellow's poem about Balder, which so transported Lewis when he was a child at Little Lea. Lewis argues: "The other longing, that for fairy land, is very different. A child does not long for fairy land as a boy longs to be the hero of the first eleven" (38). Using words similar to his description of his experience of Joy, Lewis then goes on in the essay to describe the special kind of longing a fairy tale evokes in the reader.

> It would be much truer to say that fairy land arouses a longing for he knows not what. It stirs and troubles him (to his life-long enrichment) with the dim sense of something beyond his reach and, far from dulling or emptying the actual world, gives it a new

dimension of depth. He does not despise real woods because he has read of enchanted woods: the reading makes all real woods a little enchanted.

In *The Voyage of the Dawn Treader*, Lewis describes Eustace Clarence Scrubb as a boy whose problems in many ways can be traced to the fact that he had read "only the wrong books" (87). At Wynyard, Lewis stopped reading stories about enchanted woods and instead read stories about schoolboys who became the captains of their soccer team and won the unwinnable game. This change to a steady diet of only the wrong books made Jack's actual world duller and emptier and a little less enchanted.

If we jump ahead to chapter 5 of the autobiography, where Lewis describes the return of Joy to his life, he again proposes an association between Joy and his reading, though once again exactly how they are interconnected is not fully explained. Using words that echo his statement from chapter 2, Lewis writes: "Nothing but necessity would make me reread most of the books that I read at Oldie's or at Campbell. From that point of view it is all a sandy desert. The authentic 'Joy' (as I tried to describe it in an earlier chapter) had vanished from my life: so competently that not even the memory of the desire of it remained" (72).

Farewell to Wynyard: On to Campbell

The eleven-year-old Lewis said a final good-bye to Wynyard on July 12, 1910, but it took him the rest of his life to finally let go of his resentment toward Capron. In a letter included in *Letters to an American Lady* dated July 6, 1963, a little more than four months before his death, Lewis tells his correspondent:

> Do you know, only a few weeks ago I realized suddenly that I at last *had* forgiven the cruel schoolmaster who so darkened my childhood. I'd been trying to do it for years: and like you,

each time I thought I'd done it, I found after a week or so it all had to be attempted over again. But this time I feel sure it is the real thing. And (like learning to swim or to ride a bicycle) the moment it does happen it seems so easy and you wonder why on earth you didn't do it years ago. (120)

Early in *The Lion, the Witch and the Wardrobe*, the Professor muses, "I wonder what they *do* teach them in these schools" (50). In *Surprised by Joy*, Lewis describes what he was taught at Wynyard as a sea of arithmetic and a jungle of dates, battles, imports, and exports—useless facts forgotten immediately after they were memorized. Summing up the academic setback from his two years at Wynyard, he candidly writes, "Intellectually, the time I spent at Oldie's was almost entirely wasted; if the school had not died, and if I had been left there two years more, it would probably have sealed my fate as a scholar for good" (34).

But mercifully, Wynyard did close, and in September 1910 Albert arranged to send his younger son to continue his studies at Campbell College, a school located about a mile from Little Lea. Jack would board with the other students during the week and come home on weekends. This new arrangement, Lewis notes, filled him with delight, particularly after being at Wynyard. And so it is ironic that Campbell would be the one school that his father would decide on his own to remove him from—and after less than two months.

In chapter 8 of *Surprised by Joy*, Lewis explains that his father's overall goal in sending his two sons away to boarding school was to turn them into public-school boys. Readers today, especially those who are not British, may have trouble understanding not only Albert's motivation but also what Lewis means by this statement.

Part of the problem is vocabulary. When Lewis uses the term *public school*, he means what in America would be called a private school. Malvern, the final school Lewis would attend before enrolling at Oxford, was a public school, as it was open to the paying public and so differed from the kind of private tutoring Lewis received at home and later with William Kirkpatrick. Malvern—the equivalent to an American high school—was Malvern *College* because the students lived together collegially. Adding to the confusion, universities in Great Britain are typically composed of independent, self-governing entities which are also called colleges. For example, at Oxford Lewis was part of University College. Wynyard, Campbell, and Cherbourg—the first three schools Lewis attended—were also called *prep* schools because they helped prepare boys for the entrance examination at a public school like Malvern.

The other part of the problem in understanding Albert's intentions has to do with culture. George Sayer, who was not only Lewis's friend and biographer but also senior English master at Malvern from 1949 to 1974, describes one side of Albert's fatherly desires for Jack and Warnie this way:

> He knew that a public school education would be a great advantage, even in some cases indispensable, if his sons wanted to go into the civil service or to become officers in the army or navy. In fact, as it turned out, it helped both in this way. Warren became a professional soldier, and Jack was an officer in World War I. Albert supposed that such an education would help his sons if they later wanted to go on to Oxford or Cambridge, universities that recruited their students largely from the public schools. (56)

However, if part of Albert's motive was that his two sons would have the background needed for certain careers, Sayer suggests that it was not the biggest part: "Albert's main motive was social, the desire for his sons to attain and preserve the status of gentlemen, to sound and look right, to talk without an accent, to wear the right sort of clothes, and to have good manners (that is, manners acceptable to older men of the same class)" (57).

During his two miserable years at Oldie's, Jack had begged his father to be allowed to transfer to Campbell. After Wynyard closed, Albert consented, and Jack became a Campbell student in September 1910. Two months later, in early November, Jack developed a cough and was sent home.

He would never return.

In those days, boys like Lewis who were subject to frequent coughs and colds were said to have weak chests, and doctors at the time often recommended they avoid damp or rainy climates—like the one found in Belfast. So when in January 1911 Albert sent his younger son midyear to Cherbourg School in Malvern, England, rather than back to Campbell, it perhaps was to help Jack avoid the kind of illness that had sent him home. George Sayer maintains, "No doubt Albert sent Jack to Malvern because the town had a great reputation as a health resort" (65). It is unclear whether this move had any effect on Jack's health. Near the end of his time at Cherbourg, Jack took the entrance exam for Malvern while suffering from an intense bout of the flu. In his memoir, Warnie writes, "I am inclined to rate his winning of a scholarship under these circumstances the greatest academic triumph of his career" (24).

Contributing to Jack's frequent coughs and colds was the fact that he, like his brother, had begun smoking cigarettes, a practice the brothers worked hard to hide from their father and school authorities. Lewis would smoke a pipe and cigarettes all the rest of his life, and many of the pictures of the adult Lewis show him with a cigarette in hand.

But there was another factor in Albert's decision besides Jack's health.

In chapter 3 of his autobiography, where he describes his two months at Campbell, Lewis tells us that the boys there were much more socially mixed than at most English schools. At Campbell he went to classes with the sons of farmers and tradesmen. If part of the reason Albert sent his boys to English boarding schools was to make them into upper-class English gentlemen—in accent, manners, and dress—then Campbell really would not do. Whether because of the dampness, the social mix, or both, Jack was not allowed to return even after his cough was gone.

Lewis writes in *Surprised by Joy* that the most important thing that happened during his short time at Campbell was that, thanks to an excellent English teacher, he came to love narrative verse. He does not comment about his spiritual growth during this time—growth forward or backward. He does, however, mention that the classmate he was closest to had previously gone on rounds with his father's van and kept the books, because he was the only one who could read. After leaving Campbell, Lewis would have few opportunities to rub shoulders as equals with working-class people. Following his conversion, this kind of egalitarianism became an important component of his faith. At Holy Trinity, the local church he attended, Lewis encountered the same sort of social mix he had found at Campbell.

Cherbourg House and Lewis's Loss of Belief

In chapter 4 of *Surprised by Joy*, Lewis describes his move to Cherbourg House, a preparatory school in Malvern, England, which was also the location of Malvern College, where Warnie was a student. Jack had recently turned twelve (not thirteen, as he mistakenly tells us) and would attend Cherbourg for two and a half years, from January 1911 to July 1913. During this time he would receive a very good education, one that allowed him to more than make up for his two substandard years at Wynyard.

But at Cherbourg Jack would also lose all the Christian beliefs he had previously acquired.

Lewis uses the first five lines of George's Herbert's poem "The Collar" as the chapter's epigraph.

> I struck the board and cried, "No more
> I will abroad!"
> What? shall I ever sigh and pine?
> My lines and life are free: free as the road,
> Loose as the wind, as large as store.

For thirty-two of the poem's thirty-six lines, Herbert's speaker, arguably Herbert himself, rants and raves about the confining yoke, or collar, of Christianity.

Lewis intentionally opens with a poem about rebellion and the desire to be as free as the road and loose as the wind, for in this chapter he tells how he freed himself from what Herbert in a later line calls the cage of faith. Those who are familiar with the poem—and Lewis typically assumes his readers will be as familiar as he is with the British and classical literature he quotes—know that in the last four lines the speaker's ravings grow "more fierce and wild at every word" until he hears a voice that calls him "Child." His rebellion ends in humble submission as he replies, "My Lord."

Jack grew tired of sighing and pining over the restraints he increasingly felt from Christianity. His rebellion against God would—like that of the speaker in "The Collar"—lead to more and more agitation before ultimately ending in surrender as well, but not until years after his time at Cherbourg, where he would figuratively pound on the table, Herbert's *board*, and cry, "No more!"

As Lewis opens his account of the thirty months he attended Cherbourg House, he tells us that it was there he made his first real friends. Then he interrupts his narration to announce, "But there, too, something far more important happened to me" (58). What could possibly be more important to a young boy at a new school far from home than making his first friends? Lewis tells us: "I ceased to be a Christian."

In the pages which follow, Lewis relates what he knows about the conscious reasons he abandoned his faith during this time and what he suspects about the unconscious ones.

In *The Screwtape Letters*, written a decade before *Surprised by Joy*, Lewis tells the story of a new convert and the two diabolic tempters who seek to undermine his beliefs. In the preface to the 1960 edition of *Screwtape*, Lewis explains that his insights into the ways a beginner's faith might be weakened did not, as some readers suggested, come from years of studying moral and ascetic theology. Lewis makes it clear that he had available to him an equally reliable way of understanding how temptation works: *his own experience*. In *The Screwtape Letters*, Lewis incorporates many elements from the story of how he himself ceased to be a Christian.

One of the very first instructions Screwtape gives Wormwood is that he must find a way to thwart the new convert's prayer life.

"The best thing, where it is possible," Screwtape explains, "is to keep the patient from the serious intention of praying altogether" (15). If prayer to the Enemy (the devils' term for God) cannot be prevented, Wormwood is told to fall back on subtler misdirection of his patient's attention. Screwtape explains: "Whenever they are attending to the Enemy Himself we are defeated, but there are ways of preventing them from doing so. The simplest is to turn their gaze away from Him towards themselves. Keep them watching their own minds" (16). Several pages later, Screwtape makes this part of a general rule: "In all activities favorable to the Enemy bend his mind back on itself. . . . So fix his attention inward that he no longer looks beyond himself to see our Enemy or his own neighbors" (26–27).

In chapter 4 of *Surprised by Joy*, Lewis describes how his own prayer life was impeded at Cherbourg by this kind of excessively inward focus.

> I had been told as a child that one must not only say one's prayers but think about what one was saying. Accordingly, when (at Oldie's) I came to serious belief, I tried to put this into practice. At first it seemed plain sailing. But soon the false conscience . . . came into play. One had no sooner reached "Amen" than it whispered, "Yes. But are you sure that you were really thinking about what you said?"; then, more subtly, "Were you, for example, thinking about it as well as you did last night?" (61)

In this way Jack set out in his nightly prayers to produce by sheer willpower something which willpower could and would never produce. The result of these efforts was, not surprisingly, repeated failure.

Before long, the mere thought of these endlessly inward-turning prayers cast a gloom over the entire evening, and young Jack began to dread bedtime. How exactly did Lewis's mistaken ideas contribute to his loss of faith? Lewis reports that the ludicrous burden of these false duties in prayer gave him an unconscious motive for wishing to cast off his Christian beliefs, and in this way made him more susceptible to the other temptations he encountered at Cherbourg.

In letter 9, Screwtape warns Wormwood that in his efforts to weaken the patient's faith, it is vitally important to keep him from encounters with experienced Christians who might be able to provide instruction, guidance, and correction. In *Surprised by Joy*, Lewis comments on the absence of mature spiritual guidance which he experienced at this crucial point in his own life. "If only someone had read to me old Walter Hilton's warning that we must never in prayer strive to extort 'by maistry' what God does not give!" Lewis laments. "But no one did" (62).

No one did. And so without religious direction from more-experienced Christians, young Jack was left on his own to try to master his misguided and erroneous technique of prayer "realizations," as he called them. Later, as a mature Christian, Lewis would spend countless hours—through books, talks, and thousands of letters—providing the very guidance on prayer and other matters of the faith that he himself failed to receive.

In his entry on prayer written for *The C. S. Lewis Readers' Encyclopedia*, Perry Bramlett suggests, "It is quite possible that C. S. Lewis wrote more about prayer than any other subject" (331). In one example, the essay titled "The Efficacy of Prayer," Lewis explains at length how prayer is neither magic nor a machine. Lewis continued to offer wise instruction about prayer right up until his death. In his final book, *Letters to Malcolm: Chiefly on Prayer*, we find Lewis's statement about how rare truly helpful advice on the topic can be and his implied motive for writing so much about it himself. He tells the fictional Malcolm: "My experience is the same as yours. I have never met a book on prayer which was much use to people in our position" (62).

In his autobiography, Lewis describes another occasion at Cherbourg when he lacked spiritual guidance, one which occurred as he left behind the Latin exercises he had done at Little Lea and Wynyard and began to read the classics themselves, especially Virgil. It quickly became clear to the young Lewis that his teachers and the editors of his texts simply took for granted that the religious ideas in classical literature—in this case, statements about the Roman gods and goddesses—were sheer illusion. In Jack's mind a question arose: If all the religious stories of antiquity were simply dismissed as human attempts to explain the unknown and make a hostile universe less frightening, by what means could the stories of Christianity be declared to be an exception?

Why was Christianity treated differently? he asked, never at the time receiving an answer. "Need I, at any rate, continue to treat it differently?" he began to wonder (63). This quandary became one of the conscious causes of doubt that began to assail him.

Here again Lewis points out his lack of spiritual direction during the years at Cherbourg: "No one ever attempted to show in what sense Christianity fulfilled Paganism or how Paganism prefigured Christianity" (62). Without instruction from more-experienced Christians about what made the biblical record any different from pagan myths, Lewis took the initial steps that a number of years later would lead him to conclude, as summarized here for his friend Arthur Greeves, "All religions, that is, all mythologies to give them their proper name, are merely man's own invention—Christ as much as Loki" (CLI, 230–31).

No one ever attempted to show in what sense Christianity fulfilled Paganism or how Paganism prefigured Christianity.

If during his time at Cherbourg Lewis was never told what made the stories of the supernatural we find in Christianity different from other ancient myths, we know exactly when, where, and by whom this deficiency was remedied.

Almost exactly fifteen years after writing to Greeves that all religions are merely man's own invention, Lewis would pen another, very different letter to him describing a discussion he had had with two experienced Christians as they walked and talked together late into the night. On October 18, 1931, Lewis wrote to Greeves that Hugo Dyson and J. R. R. Tolkien had explained how "the Pagan stories are God expressing Himself through the minds of poets, using such images as He found there" and how the story of Christ is "a myth working on us in the same way as the others, but with this tremendous difference that *it really happened*" (CLI, 977).

After his conversion—in part to avoid the type of spiritual missteps he made when left on his own as a schoolboy—Lewis chose to meet regularly with Walter Adams, an Anglican minister, who served as his spiritual director right up until Father Adams's death in 1952. About Father Adams, scholar Lyle Dorsett has observed that during the years he and Lewis met together, it is doubtful that anyone had "a more profound impact on Lewis's spiritual development" (88).

But, once more, we are getting ahead of ourselves.

Lewis describes a number of other factors which contributed to his loss of faith at Cherbourg—among them the deeply ingrained pessimism which had developed over his youth due to several causes, including his lack of manual dexterity. But perhaps the two biggest factors came from the influence of a non-Christian master and, ironically, from Lewis's own distinctive and deep-set desire to be enchanted.

In letter 22 of *The Screwtape Letters*, Screwtape complains to Wormwood, "Everything has to be *twisted* before it's any use to us. . . . Nothing is naturally on our side" (118–19). In the preface to *Mere Christianity*, Lewis provides an illustration of this principle, proposing that the bad impulse to gamble, something he himself was never tempted by, is an "excess or perversion" of some corresponding good impulse—which he also therefore lacked (xii). During his time at Cherbourg, the years when he was twelve and thirteen, Lewis's longing for something beyond the world, a good impulse which had contributed to his experiences of Joy at Little Lea, was twisted into an unhealthy interest in the occult.

In his autobiography, Lewis goes to great lengths to tell us that the person who helped ignite his interest in "spirits other than God and man" should not be blamed for the change it brought in his life (59). He points out that Miss C.—Lewis's name for Miss G. E. Cowie, the school matron—was still in her spiritual immaturity when she was on the staff at Cherbourg, still seeking for truth. She, too, searched without much help or religious direction, for, as Lewis reports, "Guides were even rarer then than now."

The list of strange beliefs Miss C. floundered through included theosophy, Rosicrucianism, and spiritualism. Lewis insists that in her discussions with him, she never intended to tear down his faith. But given his profound interest in, as Lewis calls it, "the preternatural," it was as though Miss C. had brought a candle into a room that was full of gunpowder.

Because he was without orthodox spiritual guidance, Lewis tells us, his hunger for something beyond this world turned into a passion for the occult. To let go of the stern truths of the creed and to embrace the vague speculations of spiritualism with nothing to be obeyed or believed except what was exciting or comforting—"Oh, the relief of it!" Lewis recalls (60).

If Miss C.'s ineptness inadvertently helped lead the young Lewis astray, another figure at Cherbourg did so with more cleverness and sophistication. In letter 10 of *The Screwtape Letters*, we learn about the desirable new acquaintances Wormwood's convert has been introduced to—desirable in that they will be another factor to help draw him away from faith. Screwtape writes that they are "just the sort of people we want him to know—rich, smart, superficially intellectual, and brightly skeptical about everything in the world" (49). In *Surprised by Joy*, Lewis describes a new teacher, Percy Harris—Lewis calls him Pogo—who came to Cherbourg. Pogo was "glossy all over"—a snazzy dresser, a real wit, and very much the man about town (67).

Lewis confesses that he soon began not only to look up to Pogo but also to emulate him: "What attracted me through Pogo was not the Flesh (I had that of my own) but the World: the desire for glitter, swagger, distinction, the desire to be in the know. . . . I began to labor very hard to make myself into a fop, a cad, and a snob" (68).

Screwtape concludes letter 12 with this guiding principle: "The safest road to Hell is the gradual one—the gentle slope, soft underfoot, without sudden turnings, without milestones, without signposts" (61). Correspondingly, in chapter 4 of *Surprised by Joy*—which Lewis ironically titles "I Broaden My Mind"—he reports, "And so, little by little, with fluctuations which I cannot now trace, I became an apostate, dropping my faith with no sense of loss but with the greatest relief" (66).

Before leaving this stage in Lewis's life, we might again look, as we did earlier, at a biographer who claims to know Lewis better than he knew himself. A. N. Wilson offers this corrected analysis of Lewis's account of his loss of faith at Cherbourg as reported to us in *Surprised by Joy*:

> We feel too strongly the presence of the middle-aged Lewis looking back on the Peter Pan, pubescent boy-Lewis and being horrified by his "loss of faith, of virtue, of simplicity." The passages, for example, where he describes his longing to abandon Christianity because of an over-scrupulous terror that he was not sufficiently concentrating on his prayers . . . are far too specifically recalled to be plausible. The details are too sharp. His saying that he hates himself for becoming at this period a "prig" and a "snob" is really another way of saying that he hates himself for having grown up at all. (28–29)

If a biographer does not believe it is possible to have an authentic faith in God—because there is no God—then he must provide an alternative account of this *so-called* faith and its loss. If this same biographer sees nothing morally wrong with self-centeredness and pride, then he will call becoming a snob and a prig during adolescence simply growing up.

As was noted earlier, there is a type of biography that takes the details Lewis gives us about his life and, using a secular lens, claims to be able to see through them to what really lies behind them in a way that Lewis himself could not. There is a type of biography that sees this practice as its proper function and purpose.

This is not that type of biography.

The End of Boyhood and the Return of Joy

Lewis titles chapter 5 of his autobiography "Renaissance." Though, as he tells us, he did not believe there had been a general cultural Renaissance as is typically described by historians, Lewis did believe in a personal renaissance—or, at least, in the possibility of one—a "wonderful reawakening which comes to most of us when puberty is complete" (71).

Alternatively, Lewis might have labeled this chapter "Recovery"— the recovery, as he notes, of "things we had in childhood and lost when we became boys" (71). Among the things recovered was the experience of Joy which Jack had known earlier as a child.

Here in chapter 5, Lewis's real-life arc of spiritual growth becomes more complicated than the fictional one he typically gives to his protagonists. He does not move on to the next stage of his life but instead presents another strand that is concurrent with the events of chapter 4. Not only does this second strand have little relation to the story told in the previous chapter, but it also runs counter to it.

Paradoxically, for Lewis this wonderful renaissance took place at the same time as his loss of faith and his transformation into a snob.

Acknowledging the difficulty that the existence of these opposing threads presents in telling his story, and knowing that his readers may find his account harder to comprehend at this point, Lewis states: "I almost have to tell two separate stories. The two lives do not seem to influence each other at all" (78).

Here again, like the experiences of the Christian mystics mentioned earlier, Lewis's spiritual experience may be hard to relate to. As a child, he was strangely transported by a few lines of a poem by Longfellow about the death of Balder. Now, after passing through the Dark Ages of boyhood, Lewis suddenly, in a flash, rediscovers this same Joy he knew years before. This time it comes not through lines from a Longfellow poem or a book by Beatrix Potter but through the sight of a headline and a picture from a literary periodical someone had left in the Cherbourg schoolroom.

Lewis writes that his long winter without Joy "broke up in a single moment" (72), and it is hard not to be reminded of the glorious return of spring in *The Lion, the Witch and the Wardrobe* after the hundred-year reign of the White Witch, when it was always winter and never Christmas. Deep layers of what Lewis refers to as "secular ice" gave way to an inner landscape filled with flowers and trees in bloom. "I can lay my hand on the very moment," Lewis writes. "There is hardly any fact I know so well, though I cannot date it."

Biographers Green and Hooper identify the literary periodical Jack saw as a Christmas issue of the *Bookman* and so date this occurrence near the start of his second year at Cherbourg, in December of 1911. The headline was for a review of Margaret Armour's recently published translation of *Siegfried and the Twilight of the Gods*. These seven words of the title and a picture Arthur Rackham had drawn for the book—just these two things—had an immediate effect on the thirteen-year-old Lewis. Quoting a line from the long poetic work *Taliessin through Logres* by his friend Charles Williams, Lewis tells us that in this moment, "The sky had turned round" (72).

Here we must again turn to Lewis's own account of the incident, told in his own words, and even then what he tells us may remain, to some extent, inscrutable.

What I had read was the words *Siegfried and the Twilight of the Gods*. What I had seen was one of Arthur Rackham's illustrations to that volume. . . . Pure "Northernness" engulfed me: a vision of huge, clear spaces hanging above the Atlantic in the endless twilight of Northern summer, remoteness, severity. . . . And with that plunge back into my past there arose at once, almost like heartbreak, the memory of Joy itself, the knowledge that I had once had what I now lacked for years, that I was returning at last from exile and desert lands to my own country. (72–73)

After this, Lewis was unable to contain his enthusiasm for all things Northern. He began to read everything he could find related to the Norse myths, he bought records of Wagner's *Ring* operas, and he even began writing a long narrative poem of his own based on the Nibelung story. In Lewis's discussion of this poem, we find something which may help us better understand his experience of Joy on seeing the seven words and the illustration.

Up until this time, Lewis tells us, if his lines rhymed, had the proper number of beats, and helped advance the plot, he was satisfied. But now, after this renewed experience of Joy after its long absence, Lewis wanted to do more. "I began to try to convey some of the intense excitement I was feeling," he explains in his autobiography, "to look for expressions which would not merely state but suggest" (74).

Expressions which would not merely state but suggest. Here readers may think back to the expression Lewis was so moved by earlier: "Balder the beautiful / Is dead, is dead."

While it is safe to say that few, if any, Lewis fans have been moved like he was by the seven words *Siegfried and the Twilight of the Gods*, they may have been moved by one of Lewis's own seven-word phrases in which he himself suggests far more than he states. Early in *The Lion, the Witch and the Wardrobe*, shortly after Peter, Susan, Edmund, and Lucy meet him, Mr. Beaver signals for them to come in closer so no one else will hear, and whispers, "They say Aslan is on the move" (67).

They say Aslan is on the move.

Even though Jack had no idea who Siegfried was when he read the words *Siegfried and the Twilight of the Gods* on the cover of the December 1911 *Bookman*, a very curious thing happened to him. Years later, in *The Lion, the Witch and the Wardrobe*, Lewis would write this passage, which comes after Mr. Beaver's statement about Aslan and reflects much of his own experience:

> And now a very curious thing happened. None of the children knew who Aslan was any more than you do; but the moment the Beaver had spoken these words everyone felt quite different. Perhaps it has sometimes happened to you in a dream that someone says something which you don't understand but in the dream it feels as if it had some enormous meaning—either a terrifying one which turns the whole dream into a nightmare or else a lovely meaning too lovely to put into words, which makes the dream so beautiful that you remember it all your life and are always wishing you could get into that dream again. It was like that now. (67–68)

In the words "any more than you do," Lewis includes his readers in the experience, making it possible for us to have the same wonderful feeling of longing that sweeps over everyone except Edmund at this point. Through the clause "They say Aslan is on the move," Lewis suggests more than he states and evokes a sensation similar to the one that came over him years before in the Cherbourg schoolroom.

One association between the story of the new convert's struggles to pray in *The Screwtape Letters* and Lewis's own struggles in *Surprised by Joy* has already been suggested, yet another interesting connection can be found. In the original preface to the 1942 *Screwtape*, Lewis writes: "There are two equal and opposite errors into which our race can fall about the devils. One is to disbelieve in their existence. The other is to believe, and to feel an excessive and unhealthy interest in them" (ix). As Lewis tells the stories of his loss of faith in chapter 4 and his renaissance and the return of Joy in chapter 5, it is clear that he believes supernatural forces—both divine and fiendish—played a role.

In describing the effect that Miss Cowie's comments about the occult had in moving him away from Christianity, Lewis tells us, "I do not mean that Miss C. did this; better say *that the Enemy did this in me*, taking occasion from things she innocently said" (60, emphasis added). He continues by pointing out, "One reason why the Enemy found this so easy was that without knowing it, I was already desperately anxious to get rid of my religion." Lewis says no more about the devil's actions here and, in this way, follows his own principle of not taking an excessive or unhealthy interest in the enemy's doings.

If Lewis comments about the enemy's role in his spiritual life, he also comments on God's role. In chapter 4, he points out that it would be inaccurate to trace his loss of virtue to the influence of Pogo. Instead, Lewis tells us, "This is amply accounted for by the age I had then reached and by my recent, in a sense, my deliberate, withdrawal of myself from Divine protection" (68). Near the end of chapter 5, Lewis reflects on the way that his interest in Norse mythology was used by God to accomplish good: "I can almost think that I was sent back to the false gods there to acquire some capacity for worship against the day when the true God should recall me to Himself" (77). While Lewis does not directly say here by whom he was sent back, we are clearly meant to see the hand of Providence at work.

Before moving on, perhaps it bears pointing out that Lewis's interest in Norse mythology was just that—an interest, a very passionate one—but *not* an actual belief. Lewis closes chapter 5 with this statement about his explosion of enthusiasm for all things Northern: "Remember that it never involved the least grain of belief: I never mistook imagination for reality" (82).

In a letter written in 1941, Lewis claims that *Centuries of Meditations* by the seventeenth-century poet and religious writer Thomas Traherne was the most beautiful book in English prose he had ever read. A decade later he would use a sentence from one of the hundreds of short meditations from this book as the epigraph for the chapter about his renaissance. In it we can find additional explanation of what the rebirth he describes in chapter 5 was really about. Here is Traherne's "Meditation 2," with the passage Lewis quotes put in italics:

> Though it be a maxim in the schools that there is no Love of a thing unknown, yet I have found that things unknown have a secret influence on the soul, and like the center of the earth unseen violently attract it. We love we know not what, and therefore everything allures us. As iron at a distance is drawn by the lodestone, there being some invisible communications between them, *so is there in us a world of Love to somewhat, though we know not what in the world that should be.* There are invisible ways of conveyance by which some great thing doth touch our souls, and by which we tend to it. Do you not feel yourself drawn with the expectation and desire of some Great Thing? (3)

Like Shasta in *The Horse and His Boy*, who states "I've been longing to go to the North all my life" though he does not know why (14), at Cherbourg Lewis felt a pull from an invisible source—like magnetism, like gravity. It was a pull that would not let go and could, like a great lodestone, draw a soul far distant, as Lewis's certainly was, to its unseen center. At the very same time as he was abandoning his faith and gradually turning into a cad and a fop, Lewis was also being drawn to something unknown he had been created to love.

Lewis's longing for Norse myth was really just, to use Traherne's phrase, a way of conveyance. The unseen, unknown "Great Thing" Lewis was being drawn to was God.

3

Young Man
and University Student

(1 9 1 3 – 1 9 2 5)

> I decided I had done with all that. No more Avalon,
>
> no more Hesperides. I had . . . "seen through" them.
>
> And I was never going to be taken in again.
>
> —*Surprised by Joy*, chapter 13

Malvern College: Bullies and the Inner Ring

"You've always liked being beastly to anyone smaller than yourself," Peter tells Edmund in chapter 5 of *The Lion, the Witch and the Wardrobe*. "We've seen that at school before now" (46). In the end, Lucy's cordial not only heals Edmund's battle wounds but also frees him from his desire to dominate and tyrannize others, a condition which had penetrated him much deeper and plagued him much longer. We are told that Lucy returns from her rounds to find Edmund looking better than she had seen him look in ages—in fact, "ever since his first term at that horrid school which was where he had begun to go wrong" (180).

The implication is that Edmund had fallen in with the bullies at his school, had lost his way, and has finally been set on the right path again.

Jack arrived at Malvern College on September 18, 1913, a little more than two months shy of his fifteenth birthday. From the start, he was, as Warnie points out in his memoir, a "square peg in a round hole" (24). This was partly due to the fact that Jack was neither good at nor interested in sports—called *games* at Malvern—and it seemed everyone else was. And it was partly due to the fact that he was keenly interested in good literature and Wagner, and it seemed everyone else was interested in magazines and ragtime. But the fact that Jack's aesthetic sensibilities were acutely out of step with those of his peers at Malvern was not his greatest problem.

Ten days after his arrival, Jack wrote home complaining that out-of-class duties and nonacademic tasks were taking up all of his study time, but expressing hope that this constant state of hurry was only temporary. He tells Albert:

> The work here is very heavy going, and it is rather hard to find time for it in the breathless life we lead here. So far that "breathlessness" is the worst feature of the place. You never get a "wink of peace." It is a perpetual rush. . . . I suppose this sense of being eternally hustled will wear off as things settle down. (*CLI*, 31)

But the perpetual rush Jack encountered at Malvern did not go away. If anything, it got worse as he encountered a system of harassment and bullying which was not the work of a few malicious students who liked to oppress their weaker classmates when teachers' backs were turned but an arrangement which was approved by the very school structure itself. At Malvern Lewis came up against a very small governing class of students in whom, as he tells us in *Surprised by Joy*, "every kind of power, privilege, and prestige" were officially united (85). This group of Bloods—as he calls them, since they made up Malvern's version of the blue-blooded aristocracy—exercised the power of command over the rest of the students, forcing them to do the group's chores, run their errands, and fetch their tea.

"When a Blood wanted his O.T.C. kit brushed and polished, or his boots cleaned, or his study 'done out,' or his tea made, he shouted," Lewis recounts (95). Unfortunately, when a Blood shouted that he wanted his Officers' Training Corps kit brushed or some other menial chore done, Jack was one of the school's peasant class who was required to come running.

What Lewis is disparaging here is the British system of fagging. While in the United States the term has come to have a different meaning, the original meaning of *fag* is any tiring or unwelcome task. In England, to be *fagged out* still means to be exhausted. In chapter 6 of *Surprised by Joy*, which Lewis titles "Bloodery," he tells readers: "No true defender of the Public Schools will believe me if I say that I was tired. But I was—dog tired, cab-horse tired, tired (almost) like a child in a factory" (96).

"Spiritually speaking," Lewis later explains, "the deadly thing was that school life was a life almost wholly dominated by the social struggle; to get on, to arrive, or, having reached the top, to remain there, was the absorbing preoccupation. It is often, of course, the preoccupation of adult life as well" (108).

This idea of an inner circle that seeks to dominate everyone else—or as Tolkien might have said, to rule them all—is a topic that Lewis returns to again and again. From this all-absorbing preoccupation to be included among those at the very top, Lewis observes, "all sorts of meanness flow" both "at school as in the world," including

> the sycophancy that courts those higher in the scale, the cultiva-
> tion of those whom it is well to know, the speedy abandonment
> of friendships that will not help on the upward path, the readi-
> ness to join the cry against the unpopular, the secret motive in
> almost every action. . . . It would perhaps not be too much to
> say that in some boys' lives everything was calculated to the
> great end of advancement.

In *That Hideous Strength*, Lewis tells the story of Mark Studdock, a sociologist obsessed with being admitted to the control-
ling, inner ring at Bracton College, where he is a fellow. After
he succeeds at this first goal, he goes on to become the writer of
dishonest newspaper articles for an even more powerful inner
ring—that of an evil organization calling itself, paradoxically,
the N.I.C.E. Mark thinks to himself "how splendid and how
triumphantly grown up" it is having all of the inner ring of the
N.I.C.E. depending on him and "nobody ever again having the
least right to consider him a nonentity or cipher" (132).

Lewis's most scathing indictment of the inner ring of bullies
endemic to the British educational system of his day can be found
in his depiction of Experiment House, the school Eustace and
Jill attend in *The Silver Chair*. Lewis revisits Professor Kirke's
concern about what is taught in schools, as the narrator reports
that learning is out of fashion and bullying is in. Readers are
told, "Owing to the curious methods of teaching at Experiment
House, one did not learn much French or Math or Latin or
things of that sort; but one did learn a lot about getting away
quickly and quietly when They were looking for one" (10–11).

Jack continued to complain to Albert throughout his time
at Malvern. In March 1914 he wrote home that the persecution
was getting more severe and harder to bear.

All the prefects detest me and lose no opportunity of venting their spite. Today, for not being able to find a cap which one gentleman wanted, I have been sentenced to clean his boots every day after breakfast for a week. . . . These brutes of illiterate, ill-managed English prefects are always watching for an opportunity to drop upon you. There is no escape from them, night or day. (*CLI*, 50)

Looking back, Warnie concludes in his memoir that Jack should never have been sent to a public school. He goes on to offer this perceptive portrait of his younger brother's abilities and disposition at this point in his life:

Already, at fourteen, his intelligence was such that he would have fitted in better among undergraduates than among schoolboys; and by his temperament he was bound to be a misfit, a heretic, an object of suspicion within the collective-minded and standardizing Public School System. He was, indeed, lucky to leave Malvern before the power of this system had done him any lasting damage. (25)

In *The Silver Chair*, Jill and Eustace manage to escape the Experiment House bullies through a door in the stone wall behind the gym, a door which, the narrator points out, was nearly always locked. In his own real-life story, Jack escaped the Bloods at Malvern through an equally unforeseen way.

Lewis titles chapter 8 of *Surprised by Joy* "Release." In the chapter's final pages, he tells us that from out of all the great unpleasantness at Malvern, "There sprang what I still reckon, by merely natural standards, the most fortunate thing that ever happened to me" (128).

What was this *most fortunate thing*—according to natural, or human, standards—that *ever* happened to Lewis? In July 1914, after just one academic year, Jack was released from the prison that Malvern had become for him, as Albert consented to allow him to resume his studies with a private tutor in September. What did Jack think about this? Lewis asks us to try to imagine waking up one morning to find that the income tax, something especially burdensome in Britain, had been completely abolished or that unrequited love had somehow totally vanished from the world.

So how did this most fortunate thing come about?

In an unforeseen turn of events, Warnie's cigarettes played the key role in Jack's good fortune.

One of the contributing factors which made Jack's year at Malvern so difficult was that Warnie was no longer there. Warnie was not there because, near the end of the previous school term, he had been caught smoking by school officials and told he would not be allowed to return. Looking for a solution, Albert had asked William Kirkpatrick, who had been his own teacher years before at Belfast's Lurgan College, to help prepare Warnie for the entrance exam to the Royal Military College at Sandhurst. Kirkpatrick did such an exceptional job that Warnie, who had turned into somewhat of a slacker at Malvern, was not only admitted, but he placed twenty-first out of 201 candidates and entered as a prize cadet.

If sending Jack to follow in Warnie's footsteps to Malvern had been an extraordinarily bad idea, following Warnie to be tutored by Kirkpatrick would prove to be an extraordinarily good one.

Great Bookham: Red Beef and Strong Beer

On September 19, 1914, two months before his sixteenth birthday, Jack went to live at Gastons, the Kirkpatricks' home in the little village of Great Bookham, some thirty miles south of London. He would live with the elderly, semiretired couple until March 1917. While the rest of Europe was rapidly being drawn into what would be called the Great War, for Jack these two and a half years studying under "Kirk" would be the happiest times in a long time. While other fifteen-year-olds would have missed the camaraderie of a school full of classmates their age, Jack was thrilled just to be, for the most part, left on his own.

In chapter 9 of his autobiography—titled "The Great Knock," one of several nicknames the Lewis family used for Kirkpatrick—Lewis writes that his new tutor was the closest thing to a purely logical entity one could meet. In their discussions, including their very first talk on the way home from the train station, Kirkpatrick refused to allow any unfounded assumption to pass unchallenged. Lewis admits that most boys would not have liked this rigid insistence on objective evidence and meticulous argumentation.

"To me," Lewis records, "it was red beef and strong beer" (136).

If at age four Lewis could insist that the entire household—including his nurse, governess, brother, and parents—call him Jacksie, it must say something that Kirkpatrick—and only Kirkpatrick, it seems—was allowed to refer to him as Clive. We find Lewis's tribute to his beloved tutor in the Narnian character Professor Kirke and in the Professor's famous exclamation in *The Lion, the Witch and the Wardrobe*: "Logic! Why don't they teach logic in these schools?" (48).

Red beef and strong beer. Lewis had found his perfect setting for learning, and it was under the Great Knock that his truly extraordinary talent began to manifest itself. Letters from Kirkpatrick to Albert, collected in the unpublished "Lewis Papers," trace the gradual recognition of one of the world's greatest writers. On January 7, 1915, just four months after Jack began his studies at Gastons, Kirkpatrick writes, "I do not think there can be much doubt as to the genuine and lasting quality of Clive's individual abilities" (*LP*, 4:279). Two months later he reports to Albert: "He has read more classics in the time than

any boy I ever had, and that too, very carefully and exactly. . . .
In the Sophoclean drama, . . . he could beat me easily in the
happy choice of words and phrases" (*LP*, 4:305). A year into his
time with Jack, Kirkpatrick confesses, "He is the most brilliant
translator of Greek plays I have ever met" (*LP*, 5:17).

Years before Jack came to study under him, the Great Knock
had been raised in the church and had even spent three years at
the Presbyterian seminary in Belfast studying for the ministry. But
shortly after seminary, Kirkpatrick left the faith and even became
hostile to religious beliefs—which he found irrational and super-
stitious. In *Surprised by Joy*, Lewis pauses to remind us that his
tutor did not turn him into an atheist. Jack's own atheistic beliefs
were already fully formed before he went to study under Kirkpatrick. What his tutor gave to him was, as he puts it, "merely fresh
ammunition for the defense of a position already chosen" (140).

In his book focusing on the mystical elements of Lewis's faith,
Into the Region of Awe, David Downing offers a description
of the fresh ammunition Jack picked up during his time with
Kirkpàtrick.

> Living with this outspokenly atheistic tutor, William Kirkpatrick,
> Lewis found his unbelief reinforced by his reading in the natural
> sciences and the social sciences. From the former he gained a
> sense that life on earth is just a random occurrence in a vast,
> empty universe. . . . From the latter he concluded that all the
> world's religions, including Christianity, could be best explained
> not as claims to truth but as expressions of psychological needs
> and cultural values. (38)

Of course, not everything Jack learned from his tutor was nec-
essarily anti-Christian. The remarkable analytical ability which
Jack developed during this time could be said to be spiritually
neutral, able to be used in any cause. Thus, at Gastons, we have
a gifted and disciplined elderly atheist providing nearly three

full academic years of rigorous one-on-one training to an even more gifted and even more disciplined young atheist, training him how to think extremely clearly and logically and how to express those thoughts with the same measure of extreme clarity and analytical precision. Years later, the converted former atheist would put this training to use in writing *Mere Christianity*, one of the most logical and eloquent articulations to date of the things Christians believe and why they believe them.

But this was yet to come.

During Jack's time at Gastons, no one could have anticipated this midlife turnaround—in fact, one would have strongly suspected Lewis to continue much as he was. On Sunday, December 6, 1914, four months after beginning his tutoring, Jack went home to St. Mark's to commit what he confesses in his autobiography to be "one of the worst acts of my life" (161). Fearing to speak up against his father's wishes, Jack, a confirmed atheist, was confirmed as a full member of the Church of Ireland. "Cowardice drove me into hypocrisy," Lewis reports, "and hypocrisy into blasphemy."

In his memoir, Warnie argues that Jack's time with the Great Knock was crucial in developing his brother's unique talents and that it set the course for the rest of his life. Warnie writes, "The stimulation of a sharp and vigorous mind, . . . the ordered security of Jack's life, his freedom to read widely and gratuitously—these factors combined to develop his particular gifts and determine his future" (25–26).

Lewis begins chapter 9 with this epigraph taken from Lord Chesterfield's *Letters to His Son*: "You will often meet with characters in nature so extravagant, that a discreet poet would not venture to set them upon the stage" (132). Perhaps Lewis chose this passage simply intending that the readers of *Surprised by Joy* see Kirkpatrick as an extravagant and eccentric character—as certainly he was.

However, if we look at the sentences which come right before the section Lewis quotes, a different way to read the epigraph emerges. Here is the passage where Lord Chesterfield tells his son about people who have this extravagant nature. The part used by Lewis is in italics, and readers may notice that he has changed *dramatist* to *poet*. Lord Chesterfield makes the following observations about these unique people:

> They cannot see people suffer without sympathizing with, and endeavoring to help them. They cannot see people want without relieving them, though truly their own circumstances cannot very well afford it. They cannot help speaking truth, though they know all the imprudence of it. In short, they know that, with all these weaknesses, they are not fit to live in the world, much less to thrive in it. But they are now too old to change, and must rub on as well as they can. This sounds too ridiculous and outré, almost, for the stage; and yet, take my word for it, you will frequently meet with it upon the common stage of the world. And here I will observe, by the bye, that *you will often meet with characters in nature so extravagant, that a discreet dramatist would not venture to set them upon the stage* in their true and high coloring. (128)

William Kirkpatrick certainly spoke the truth without worrying whether or not it was prudent. And by the time Jack came to live at Gastons, the Great Knock was certainly too old to change. Lewis ends the chapter with a moving confession: "My debt to him is very great, my reverence to this day undiminished" (148). He may well have intended the epigraph which opens the chapter to introduce readers to someone who was not merely eccentric but a man who endeavored to help others, in this case two young men from Belfast—sons of an old friend who for very different reasons were in desperate need of a very special tutor.

Kirkpatrick died at Gastons on March 22, 1921, nine days before Jack would receive a first from Oxford in Classical Honor

Moderations in Greek and Latin, subjects he had been trained in by Kirk. Lewis would go on to earn two other first degrees, a spectacular achievement. In a letter written in response to his father's telegram with the sad news, Jack tried to sum up what the Great Knock had given him:

> Poor old Kirk! What shall one say of him? It would be a poor compliment to that memory to be sentimental: indeed, if it were possible he would himself return to chide the absurdity. It is no sentiment, but plainest fact to say that I at least owe to him in the intellectual sphere as much as one human being can owe another. That he enabled me to win a scholarship is the least that he did for me. It was an atmosphere of unrelenting clearness and rigid honesty of thought that one breathed from living with him— and this I shall be the better for as long as I live. (*CLI*, 534–35)

Arthur Greeves: You Like That Too?

Lewis reports that after moving in with the Kirkpatricks, he quickly settled into a fixed routine that suited him perfectly, so perfectly that he confesses to us in *Surprised by Joy*, "If I could please myself I would always live as I lived there" (141).

Jack's ideal day would begin with breakfast at exactly eight and would have him at his desk reading or writing by nine. Except for a ten-minute break for a cup of—as he makes a point of telling us—*good* tea or coffee at around eleven, he would work without interruption until precisely one o'clock, when lunch would be on the table. After lunch there would be a daily walk outdoors, typically alone so he could better take in the sounds and the silences of the natural world. The walk would end and the afternoon tea be served each day at precisely the same time, no later than four fifteen. This would be proper British tea that included something to eat—again, preferably in solitude—with something suitable to read, meaning the kind of book that could be started and stopped anywhere. Then Jack would be back at his desk for more work from five until seven. The day would conclude with the evening meal and conversation, with bedtime at eleven.

But where on this schedule was there time for him to respond to all the letters he received? Lewis reminds us that he is describing an *ideal* day, and on his ideal day he would receive almost no mail and so have no reason to dread the postman's knock. Later in life, including during the time he was writing *Surprised by Joy*, Lewis would frequently have to spend two or more hours a day replying to readers from all over the world who had written him with questions, comments, or requests for advice—a chore that was, with few exceptions, burdensome and tedious but one he felt duty-bound to perform.

Since Warnie had at this point been called up for active duty, correspondence from him came only infrequently. Lewis describes how, during his time at Gastons, he regularly received and answered only two letters a week. One, from his father, was a duty. The other, from his new friend in Belfast, was the week's highlight. The two boys had just recently met when Jack, who had purposely avoided the task up to then, was finally persuaded to pay a visit to Arthur Greeves. Arthur, who was chronically ill and lived nearby, had sent a message saying that he was in bed again convalescing and would welcome some company.

In *The Four Loves*, Lewis includes a section titled "Friendship," where he proposes:

> Friendship arises out of mere Companionship when two or more of the companions discover that they have in common some insight or interest or even taste which the others do not share and which, till that moment, each believed to be his own unique treasure (or burden). The typical expression of opening Friendship would be something like, "What? You too? I thought I was the only one." (65)

What Lewis does not say in *The Four Loves* is that this passage was drawn directly from his first meeting with Arthur, a meeting described in delightful detail in *Surprised by Joy*. What was this common interest that Jack and Arthur shared? When Jack entered Arthur's room, he was astonished to see a copy of H. A. Guerber's *Myths of the Norsemen* on the table beside Arthur. The two boys not only liked the same thing, Lewis recalls, but they liked the same parts of it and liked them in the same way.

Except for his father and his brother, there would be no one Lewis would write to more over the course of his life than Arthur. Two hundred ninety-six letters, spanning the years 1914 to 1963, in full or in part, appear in *The Letters of C. S. Lewis to Arthur Greeves*. The first letter was written while Jack was finishing his last weeks at Malvern. With the second letter, written just a week after Jack arrived at Gastons, we see their friendship begin to blossom. In this second letter Jack tells his new friend, "After a week's trial I have come to the conclusion that I am going to have the time of my life" (49), and urges Arthur to write back as soon as possible.

In the description of Arthur which Jack penned for the unpublished *Lewis Papers*, we find not only Lewis's portrait of Arthur but also an accurate portrayal of his own spiritual condition at that time.

> During the earlier years of our acquaintance he was (as always) a Christian, and I was an atheist. But though (God forgive me) I bombarded him with all the thin artillery of a seventeen-year-old rationalist, I never made any impression on his faith. . . . He remains a victor in that debate. It is I who have come round. . . . It might seem that I had much to give him, and that he had nothing to give me. But this is not the truth. I could give concepts, logic, facts, arguments, but he had feelings to offer, feelings which most mysteriously—for he was always very inarticulate—he taught me to share. Hence, in our commerce, I dealt in superficies, but

he in solids. I learned charity from him and failed, for all my efforts, to teach him arrogance in return. (*LP*, 10.218–20)

In *Surprised by Joy*, Lewis explains that besides learning charity from Arthur, he also gained an appreciation for what Arthur called the "homely"—Arthur's way of seeing beauty in the commonplace: a row of cabbages in the garden, a cat squeezing under a barn door, coals glowing in the fireplace. Before meeting Arthur, Lewis confesses that his own feelings were too narrow, as he looked for only the majestic and awe-inspiring. Mountains and sky were his special favorites, he notes. Arthur helped open him to appreciate the very qualities that he had previously disregarded. "But for him I should never have known the beauty of the ordinary vegetables that we destine to the pot," Lewis records (157). "Often he recalled my eyes from the horizon just to look through a hole in a hedge."

If during this time Arthur played a major role in helping Jack to see the world differently, there would be another big factor. This second influence came from an author who had died a decade earlier and came about because Jack just happened to pick up a book from a used-book stall while waiting for a train.

Phantastes and the Sacramental Ordinary

In *The Silver Chair*, Puddleglum, speaking for Lewis, rejects the Green Lady's claim that her dark, gloomy underground world is the only world there is, declaring: "Then all I can say is that, in that case, the made-up things seem a good deal more important than the real ones. Suppose this black pit of a kingdom of yours *is* the only world. Well, it strikes me as a pretty poor one" (182).

In chapter 11 of *Surprised by Joy*, Lewis describes a similar distinction within himself. He notes that during his Great

Bookham days, his imagination and his intellect stood in sharp contrast. On one side was a "many-islanded sea of poetry and myth," and on the other a rationalism that he found to be "glib and shallow" (170). "Nearly all that I loved I believed to be imaginary," Lewis reports. "Nearly all that I believed to be real I thought grim and meaningless."

"And then, on top of this, in superabundance of mercy," Lewis continues, "came that event which I have already more than once attempted to describe in other books. . . . The evening that I now speak of was in October" (178–79).

The other books Lewis refers to here are *The Great Divorce* and *George MacDonald: An Anthology*—both published in 1946, nine years before *Surprised by Joy*. This event of superabundant mercy actually took place in March, not October—specifically, on the evening of Saturday, March 4, 1916. We know this because we have a letter Lewis wrote to Arthur from Gastons dated March 7, 1916, in which he tells him about an amazing new book he had just bought seemingly by accident.

> I have had a great literary experience this week. I have discovered yet another author to add to our circle—our very own set. . . . The book, to get to the point, is George MacDonald's "Faerie Romance," *Phantastes*, which I picked up by hazard . . . on our station bookstall last Saturday. . . . Whatever the book you are reading now, you simply MUST get this at once. (*CLI*, 169–70)

Jack, in his routine of regular afternoon rambles, had walked the three miles or so from Great Bookham to the next village, Leatherhead, a trek he made about once a week, and was waiting for the train to take him back. He was seventeen-and-a-half at the time and had been studying at Gastons for two years, with one more still to come. Standing on the platform in the waning light, he picked a worn book from the station's used-book stall. He had seen it on previous walks to Leatherhead but had always put it back. Just as the train arrived, this time he decided to buy it.

In the preface to *George MacDonald: An Anthology*, Lewis remembers the event and the effect the book had on him.

> It must be more than thirty years ago that I bought—almost unwillingly, for I had looked at the volume on that bookstall and rejected it on a dozen previous occasions—the Everyman edition of *Phantastes*. A few hours later I knew that I had crossed a great frontier. I had already been waist-deep in romanticism. . . . Now *Phantastes* was romantic enough in all conscience; but there was a difference. Nothing was at that time further from my thoughts than Christianity and I therefore had no notion what this difference really was. . . . The whole book had about it a sort of cool, morning innocence, and also, quite unmistakably, a certain quality of Death, *good* Death. What it actually did to me was to convert, even to baptize (that was where the Death came in) my imagination. It did nothing to my intellect nor (at the time) to my conscience. Their turn came far later and with the help of many other books and men. (xxxii–xxxiii)

As noted, Lewis also comments on this life-changing event in *The Great Divorce*, where he includes himself as one of the characters who is taken on a bus ride to the outskirts of heaven. As each visitor is greeted by the "Solid Person" specially chosen to serve as his or her guide—much as Dante had Virgil as his guide in *The Divine Comedy*—Lewis encounters the Scottish clergyman and author George MacDonald. Lewis, as the first-person narrator, offers us this report of their meeting, slightly underestimating his age at the time—perhaps because in his mind this incident occurred the previous October.

> I tried, trembling, to tell this man all that his writing had done for me. I tried to tell how a certain frosty afternoon at Leatherhead Station when I first bought a copy of *Phantastes* (being then about sixteen years old) had been to me what the first sight of

Beatrice had been to Dante: *Here begins the New Life*. I started to confess how long that Life had delayed in the region of imagination merely: how slowly and reluctantly I had come to admit that his Christendom had more than an accidental connection with it, how hard I had tried not to see that the true name of this quality which first met me in his books is Holiness. (65)

In *Surprised by Joy*, Lewis tells us that up until his discovery of *Phantastes*, each visitation of Joy had left the world "momentarily a desert" (181). After each of the reminders of another world that Joy provided, Lewis tells us, "I did not like the return to ours." But the holiness—Lewis initially thought of it as a bright shadow, not recognizing it as holiness at the time—that flowed from MacDonald's story produced a fundamentally different experience of Joy. Lewis explains: "But now I saw the bright shadow coming out of the book into the real world and resting there, transforming all common things and yet itself unchanged. Or, more accurately, I saw the common things drawn into the bright shadow."

Back in chapter 5, Lewis reports that his early appreciation of nature was largely "parasitic" (77), meaning that he experienced Joy through nature only as he imagined a mountain or meadow as the setting for a scene from *Siegfried* or a Wagnerian opera. Young readers whose backyard was transformed when they pretended it was Narnia, or who saw a mouse or badger and pretended it to be Reepicheep or Trufflehunter, will understand how this works. But after reading *Phantastes*, Lewis tells us that nature—because he could now see the holiness infused into each individual natural element—became a medium of Joy by itself.

To some readers, Lewis's account of the bright shadow of holiness associated with *Phantastes* may seem nearly as incomprehensible as his previous mystical experiences. George Sayer offers this summary of the book's effect:

The influence of *Phantastes* on Jack lasted for many years, perhaps all his life. Because it was greatest at psychic depths of which he was only partly aware, he was at a loss to give a clear account of it. . . . It had a transforming influence on his attitude toward the ordinary, common things around him, imbuing them with its own spiritual quality. (107–8)

In *The Voyage of the Dawn Treader*, Eustace tells Ramandu, who in Narnia is a star at rest, "In our world, a star is a huge ball of flaming gas" (209). Ramandu corrects him, stating, "Even in your world, my son, that is not what a star is but only what it is made of." MacDonald provided Jack a similar intimation that people and things in our world cannot be reduced to just atoms and molecules.

Rather than being left with a world that had become a desert he did not want to return to, now Jack was able to see the bright light of holiness that bathed—that had always bathed, and that continued to bathe—all common things. If Arthur had helped him to see the beautiful in the ordinary, MacDonald helped him to see the holy or sacramental aspect in everything and every person—the sacramental ordinary. As Lewis tells us: "It was as though the voice which had called to me from the world's end were now speaking at my side. It was with me in the room, or in my own body, or behind me" (180).

Writing about the converted Lewis, Sayer maintains that the most precious moments to Jack were those when he was aware "of the spiritual quality of material things, of the infusion of the supernatural into the workaday world" (317).

Near the end of the *Phantastes* episode of *Surprised by Joy*, Lewis quotes the Latin phrase *unde hoc mihi?* (181). This question comes from the Vulgate version of Luke 1:43, "Et unde hoc mihi ut veniat mater Domini mei ad me?" which is Elizabeth's response when Mary enters her home, miraculously pregnant with the incarnate Son of God: "But why am I so favored, that the mother of my Lord should come to me?"

"But why am I so favored?" Lewis asks about this experience—his own version of Elizabeth's encounter—of being enabled, through MacDonald's writing, to see the divine manifest in the everyday things around him: in the bread on the table and the coals in the grate, and shining, as he reports, "on my own past life, and even on the quiet room where I sat and on my old teacher where he nodded about his little *Tacitus*" (180–81).

"But why am I so favored?" Lewis asks about being able to perceive the sacramental aspect—the holiness—in ordinary people and things. He points to the answer in the chapter's title and epigraph.

Lewis titles chapter 11 "Check" and opens it with this line—
When bale is at highest, boote is at next—from the medieval poem "Sir Aldingar." In this chapter, Lewis informs us that he tried his best to become a strict materialist who believed in nothing but "atoms and evolution and military service" (174). But his attempts were thwarted—checked, he tells us—by the seemingly accidental discovery of a worn copy of a used book which had come to be shelved in the Leatherhead Station bookstall.

So did Jack happen on the book by *hazard* on that frosty March evening in 1916, as he claimed in his letter to Arthur? Looking back, the adult Lewis suggests that this event in his life was more like part of the careful strategy of a chess player than a random accident. Three chapters later Lewis will report, "My Adversary began to make His final moves" (216), moves which will lead, as the chapter title indicates, to a final checkmate. Here in chapter 11, Lewis recounts one of the earlier moves that helped set the board for what was to come. And while Lewis will refer to God as his adversary, this will be a strangely benevolent adversary, one who has Jack's best interests in mind. Lewis's epigraph "When bale is at highest, boote is at next" may be paraphrased as "When evil is at its greatest, help is at its closest."

What was the source of this help? If we turn to chapter 4 of *Phantastes*, we find that before Lewis used this epigraph, Mac-Donald used it himself, though in a slightly different variation ("When bale is att hyest, boote is nyest"). By repeating Mac-Donald's epigraph in *Surprised by Joy*, Lewis makes it clear that the help he is referring to came from MacDonald's book.

"I have never concealed the fact that I regarded him as my master," Lewis declares in the preface to *George MacDonald: An Anthology*. "Indeed, I fancy I have never written a book in which I did not quote from him" (xxxii).

But who put the book in his way and in doing so put Jack's plan to be a strict materialist in check? Not chance or hazard, as Jack first thought, but a strategic opponent whose every move was made with intention—the intention to help and avail.

In *Surprised by Joy*, Lewis wraps up the section on his first encounter with MacDonald with these sentences: "That night my imagination was, in a certain sense, baptized; the rest of me, not unnaturally, took longer. I had not the faintest notion what I had let myself in for by buying *Phantastes*" (181).

First Taste of Oxford

Despite having lived in central England as a student since the time he was nine—at Wynyard, Cherbourg, Malvern, and Gastons—and although there were relatively easy train connections from all these places, the first time that Jack visited Oxford was when he traveled there from Great Bookham to take the university scholarship exam. The year was 1916. Lewis had just turned eighteen. The exam would last several days, from December 5 to 9.

In *Surprised by Joy*, Lewis reports that his very first taste of Oxford was comical. Upon getting off the train at the Oxford rail station, a small suitcase borrowed from Mrs. Kirkpatrick in hand, Jack headed into town looking for a place to stay. As he walked on and on, the streets became more and more shabby, with one dingy shop after another. Where was the city of dreaming spires that Matthew Arnold described? "But still I went on," Lewis writes, "always expecting the next turn to reveal the beauties" (184).

Only when it became obvious that he was coming to open country and there was no town left did Jack stop and turn around. Then he saw the city in all its glory, with its grand collection of towers and spires reaching toward the sky, a picture of academic splendor unsurpassed anywhere in the world. Jack went back in the opposite direction, first retracing his steps to the train station and then heading off in the right way. And so he finally entered the magnificent city. Lewis concludes, "I did not see to what extent this little adventure was an allegory of my whole life" (184).

In a letter written from Oxford several days after his arrival, Jack told his father, "The place has surpassed my wildest dreams: I never saw anything so beautiful" (*CLI*, 262).

I did not see to what extent this little adventure was an allegory of my whole life.

Lewis spent the first half of his life headed in the wrong direction, living in a purely materialistic world and pursuing goals that he found shallow, grim, and meaningless. Nevertheless, he kept going in this wrong direction until he was virtually forced to turn around. Only then did he see the glorious realm he had missed, the magnificent place that had been waiting for him where he could have been living all the time.

Years after his comical introduction to Oxford, perhaps with this event in mind, Lewis would write in *Mere Christianity*: "We all want progress. But progress means getting nearer to the place where you want to be. And if you have taken a wrong turning, then to go forward does not get you any nearer. If you are on the wrong road, progress means doing an about-turn and walking back to the right road" (28).

As Jack strolled along the streets of Oxford on that initial visit in December 1916, he was filled with dreams that he would be chosen from among the many highly talented candidates to receive one of the few scholarships available and would return as a university student. He also had dreams which extended beyond being an Oxford student to the next step of becoming a member of the Oxford faculty. In his autobiography, Lewis comments, "I knew very well by now that there was hardly any position in the world save that of a don in which I was fitted to earn a living, and that I was staking everything on a game in which few won and hundreds lost" (183).

As he saw for the first time the famous colleges and other landmarks he had previously only read about, the eighteen-year-old must have walked past the great University Church of St. Mary the Virgin on the north side of High Street and perhaps even stopped in to look around. But even in his wildest dreams, Jack could not have foreseen that twenty-five years later, in the midst of a second world war, he would climb the stairs to St. Mary's elevated pulpit and preach a sermon he would call "The Weight of Glory." In that sermon, perhaps remembering the worldly aspirations of his first visit, Lewis would talk about living our lives in a dismal slum instead of at the splendid seaside, telling the packed church, "We are half-hearted creatures, fooling about with drink and sex and ambition when infinite joy is offered us, like an ignorant child who wants to go on making mud pies in a slum because he cannot imagine what is meant by the offer of a holiday at the sea" (26).

The scholarship exams were administered that frigid December in the great hall of Oriel College, where Jack joined a room full of candidates who wrote their essays while still wearing their overcoats, scarves, and gloves. Though he was convinced he had done poorly and told his father so, Jack did exceptionally well on the exam and shortly before Christmas received a letter from the master of University College telling him he had been awarded one of the college's three open scholarships in classics.

"Like much else at Oxford, the entrance procedure is odd," writes George Sayer, a graduate of the system (116). Sayer explains:

> Although Jack's scholarship, a much-coveted distinction, entitled him to free rooms in his college and a grant of money toward his expenses there, it did not give him entrance to the university itself (his college was a semi-independent unit of Oxford). To gain admission to Oxford, he would have to pass a separate exam called Responsions. . . . For most boys of scholarship standard, Responsions was little more than a formality, an exam for which it was not necessary to work. But this was not true in Jack's case.

Unfortunately for Jack, the exam included a mathematics section, a subject in which Jack was notoriously weak.

Knowing of the math requirement on the responsions, Jack returned after the Christmas holidays to Great Bookham and tried to improve his dreadful math skills. But where his mother Flora had been exceptionally gifted, Jack was sensationally inept. When he went back to Oxford in March for the test, he got plowed, as he reports in his autobiography. Despite this failure, Jack was provisionally admitted and allowed to move into University College on April 26, 1917, where he stayed for a brief time before joining the Officers' Training Corps. During this interlude, he worked again on his algebra, only to fail the test for a second time in June.

With this second failure, it became clear that Lewis's deficiencies in math were far more serious than anyone had admitted, and the world came very close to losing C. S. Lewis as a scholar, teacher, and writer. Sayer comments: "He was allowed to attend Oxford after the war only because the passing of Responsions was waived for men who had been in the service. If it had not been for this piece of academic generosity, Jack would probably never have passed and never been able to make a career at Oxford or any other British university" (118).

On June 8, 1917, after less than eight weeks at University College—during which he did little more than read on his own, become familiar with Oxford, and work some on his math—Jack officially joined the British Army and was sent across town to be billeted in Keble College, which had become the quarters for the Officers' Training Corps. On the night of November 17, after what would today be considered scandalously little training and a month's leave to say what could very well be his final good-byes, Jack boarded a troop transport ship at Southampton harbor and crossed the English Channel to France.

The Great War

On November 29, 1917, Second Lieutenant Clive Staples Lewis arrived in the trenches at the front line. It was his nineteenth birthday.

Lewis devotes just one short chapter of *Surprised by Joy* to his war experience. There are several reasons for this. First, the period of time the chapter covers is relatively short. Arriving in November, Jack was sent back to England the following May after being wounded by a misguided English shell, which meant he was in France for only six months. For more than two of these months, he was in a hospital on the coast—in February recovering from trench fever, and in April and May being treated for his shrapnel wounds. Second, Lewis notes that the war itself had already been described by many others who had seen more of it than he did. Finally, while he felt the need to report on a handful of events from this time period, since they were connected to his account of how he passed from atheism to Christianity, Lewis concludes, "The rest of my war experiences have little to do with this story" (197). And so he says nothing about these other unrelated incidents.

Lewis titles the wartime chapter of his autobiography "Guns and Good Company." To his great surprise, Jack did not dislike the army as much as he thought he would. In fact, the company was far better than he had experienced at Malvern four years earlier, the last time he had been part of a large group. Being Lewis, he offers several speculations on why this was so. First, unlike at Malvern, no one in the army had to pretend that he liked it. "Straight tribulation is easier to bear," Lewis explains, "than tribulation which advertises itself as pleasure" (188). Where Jack found that the hardship at Malvern had led to distrust, deceit, and resentment, the hardship of the army created camaraderie and fondness between the fellow sufferers. Second, in noting the goodwill extended to him by his military elders, Lewis comments, "Thirty is naturally kinder to nineteen than nineteen is to thirteen."

Third, Lewis suggests that something about the look on his face had changed since his time at Malvern, where it had gotten him into a good deal of trouble. At Malvern Jack sometimes appeared insolent or disrespectful. He now had a look that elicited pity or kindly amusement. And what had brought about this change for the better? Lewis speculates that perhaps it was his reading of *Phantastes*.

In chapter 5 of *The Voyage of the Dawn Treader*, when Eustace—who is not yet on the other side of his great change—finds climbing a steep hill to be less difficult than he thought, the narrator reports that, even though Eustace did not realize it, his new life in Narnia "had already done him some good" (79). At nineteen Jack was likewise a long way from his conversion, but his Christian reading had already brought about some good in him.

Lewis found good company and goodwill not only with his fellow officers in the officers' club but also with his battalion in the trenches. Lewis reports that it was there amid the shared adversity of winter, water, warfare, and weariness that he came to "know and pity and reverence the ordinary man" (196). Years later, in "The Weight of Glory," Lewis would conclude:

> It is a serious thing to live in a society of possible gods and goddesses, to remember that the dullest and most uninteresting person you can talk to may one day be a creature which, if you saw it now, you would be strongly tempted to worship. . . . There are no *ordinary* people. You have never talked to a mere mortal. . . . Next to the Blessed Sacrament itself, your neighbor is the holiest object presented to your senses. (45–46)

This extraordinary reverence for so-called ordinary men was first learned by Second Lieutenant Lewis during the six months he lived and fought alongside them.

Jack spent the month of February in a hospital miles away from the front, recovering from the flu-like symptoms of trench fever. While there, he read a volume of essays by G. K. Chesterton. As with *Phantastes*, this discovery was made by accident, or, Lewis might say, by so-called accident. When Jack picked up Chesterton's book, he had never heard of the author and had no idea of his strong religious beliefs. If Jack had known of Chesterton's Christian faith, would he still have read the volume of essays he found while convalescing at Le Treport? Perhaps. Something had happened to him when he read *Phantastes* two years earlier—something that changed not only the look on his face but also the openness of his heart. About his first encounter with Chesterton, Lewis writes, "Strange as it may seem, I liked him for his goodness" (191).

If in his autobiography Lewis recalls that he found *holiness* in reading George MacDonald and *goodness* in reading Chesterton, we must remember that these are the names he gives to these aspects looking back years after the fact and years after his conversion. When Jack first read *Phantastes* and the book of Chesterton essays, he did not believe there was such a thing as holiness and meant something very different by the term *goodness* than he later would.

Lewis concludes with one of the more memorable passages from *Surprised by Joy*: "In reading Chesterton, as in reading MacDonald, I did not know what I was letting myself in for. A young man who wishes to remain a sound atheist cannot be too careful of his reading" (191). At the end of chapter 14, Lewis writes, "And so the great Angler played his fish" (211). If Lewis was hooked earlier by reading *Phantastes*, reading Chesterton while he convalesced in France helped to further set the hook.

In *The Screwtape Letters*, Screwtape cautions Wormwood not to hope for too much from the outbreak of war because it has "certain tendencies inherent in it" which are not in the devils' favor (23). Lewis tells us that during the time he served in France, he was assailed by good books and good men. "There are traps everywhere," he observes (191). And Jack's assailant was very ready to use all of them. Lewis makes it clear who this assailant was, as he finishes with the statement, "God is, if I may say it, very unscrupulous."

Though an armistice was signed which took effect November 11, 1918—in the eleventh hour of the eleventh day of the eleventh month—troubling memories of the Great War stayed with Jack for a long time. In a letter to Dom Bede Griffiths near the start of World War II, Lewis would write, "My memories of the last war haunted my dreams for years. . . . I think death would be much better than to live through another war" (*CLII*, 258).

Lewis was never a pacifist, but in his fictional works he never suggested that war was not terrifying or brutal. Before his battle with the wolf in *The Lion, the Witch and the Wardrobe*, Peter feels like he is going to be sick. Lewis describes the encounter as "a horrible, confused moment like something in a nightmare," where everything is "blood and heat and hair" (132).

One Huge and Complex Episode

In chapter 13 of *Surprised by Joy*, Lewis tells us that by January 1919 he was recovered from his blighty (a wound serious enough to send him back to England but not serious enough to be life threatening), demobbed (officially retired from military service), and back in Oxford to resume—or, in some ways, to start—his studies. Then, before going on with his story, he interjects four odd sentences:

> Before I say anything of my life there I must warn the reader that one huge and complex episode will be omitted. I have no choice about this reticence. All I can or need say is that my earlier hostility to the emotions was very fully and variously avenged. But even were I free to tell the story, I doubt if it has much to do with the subject of the book. (198)

The story Lewis omits here is the story of his relationship with Mrs. Janie Moore, the mother of Paddy Moore, his roommate during officers' training. In the few weeks before shipping to the front, Jack had spent time with Paddy's mother and sister, who provided the cheer and comfort that was lacking from Albert. Knowing that death was a real possibility, Jack and Paddy made a pact that if only one of them made it back, the survivor would care for the other's parent. Paddy was killed. After Jack returned to Oxford, his relationship with Mrs. Moore, presumably the source of the "emotions" Lewis alludes to in the passage, became that of an adopted son taking care of an increasingly needy adopted mother.

When Lewis reports that their relationship, which lasted thirty-two years, did not have much to do with the subject of how he passed from atheism to Christianity, we must agree with him. But it certainly had a great deal to do with his growth from new Christian to mature Christian, for in the years to come, Mrs. Moore, who was hostile to his faith, would grow very difficult to live with. Under her chronic nagging and petty demands that he do a multitude of chores around the house, Lewis would learn much about patience, humility, fortitude, and hope. No doubt one reason Jack was able to remain so faithful in his promise to Paddy was that he saw Mrs. Moore's domestic demands on him for what they really were. Given his own general ineptitude in the kitchen and dining room and his adopted mother's growing isolation from her daughter and her increasing loneliness, her requests were better understood as appeals for attention and company, appeals which Jack would have viewed with compassion and believed it his Christian duty to respond to.

Besides, of course, the promise he had made to Paddy, another reason Jack was drawn to Mrs. Moore was that when Jack really needed his father, Albert had proved unresponsive. Despite his son's requests, Albert did not come to England to see him—for what might have been their last meeting—before he shipped off to France. Nor did Albert come to visit Jack as he finished recuperating in London. About the factors behind their father's unfatherly behavior, Warnie writes in his memoir:

> My father was a very peculiar man in some respects: in none more than in an almost pathological hatred of taking any step which involved a break in the dull routine of his daily existence. Jack remained unvisited, and was deeply hurt at a neglect which he considered inexcusable. Feeling himself to have been rebuffed by his father, he turned to Mrs. Moore as to a mother,

seeking there the affection which was apparently denied him at home. 30)

In 1931 Jack, Warnie, and Mrs. Moore bought the Kilns, a house and wooded grounds just outside of Oxford. They lived there along with Mrs. Moore's daughter, Maureen, and one or two servants. Over the years, Mrs. Moore became not only increasingly difficult but also increasingly ill. By 1947, when Lewis was asked to join a prestigious group of thinkers and leaders to discuss the future of the Anglican Church, he could not give them a firm commitment, explaining: "My time is almost fully, and what is new, quite unpredictably, occupied by my domestic duties. My mother is old and infirm, we have little and uncertain help, and I never know when I can, even for a day, get away from my duties as a nurse and a domestic servant" (*CLII*, 766).

In a passage from his diary, Warnie remarks on Mrs. Moore's death in January 1951: "And so ends the mysterious self-imposed slavery in which Jack has lived for at least thirty years. How it began, I suppose I shall never know" (264).

And so would end one huge and complex episode in Jack's life.

Oxford Student Again

It is somewhat difficult to explain Jack's Oxford studies in terms non-Oxonians can understand. As was seen in describing his earlier education, again part of the problem is terminology. In mid-January 1919, in what is called Hilary term, Jack began his undergraduate work in earnest. Fourteen months later—on March 31, 1920—he was awarded a first in Classical Honor Moderations. Approximately two and a half years after this—on August 4, 1922—he was awarded an additional first in Greats. For each of these degrees, Jack had a tutor he met with once a week, a set of lectures to attend, a long list of readings, and a huge final exam. Lewis scholar and Cambridge graduate John Bremer describes the rationale behind the academic track Jack chose to follow.

> He could have proceeded directly to a degree in Greats, the popular name for the Honors School of *Literae Humaniores*, a course devoted to the classics, philosophy, and ancient history. But he thought he wanted a scholarly career, and for him that meant obtaining a fellowship at Oxford. He had confided this ambition to his tutor, A. B. Poynton, who had recommended that instead of proceeding directly to Greats he should begin with the Honor Moderations course in Greek and Latin. . . . This would give him a firmer grounding in the field of classics and a better chance to show his worth. (32)

The fellowship Bremer refers to here is a teaching position. An Oxford don is also known as a tutor or fellow. Bremer further notes, "Oxford and Cambridge undergraduates were classified as achieving First, Second, or Third Class degrees; the number of Firsts awarded was extremely small" (33).

A double first was usually the ticket to an academic career. But in 1922 the supply-and-demand ratio for academic jobs was similar to the current one, as there were far more graduates than there were university positions available, particularly positions at prestigious schools like Oxford. And so, when no position was forthcoming, like many of today's graduates Jack decided to stay in school and get another degree. In *Surprised by Joy*, he explains: "In the summer of 1922 I finished Greats. As there were no philosophical posts going, or none that I could get, my long-suffering father offered me a fourth year at Oxford during which I read English so as to get a second string to my bow" (212).

Part of Jack's strategy in going for this third degree was the diminishing prominence of classical and philosophical studies and the foreseeable rise in English literature studies. In a letter dated May 18, 1922, as he was finishing Greats, Jack writes to his father:

> No one quite knows what place classics and philosophy will hold in the educational world. . . . English Literature is a "rising" subject. Thus if I could take a First or even a Second in Greats, *and* a First next year in English Literature, I should be in a very strong position indeed: and during the extra year I might reasonably hope to strengthen it further by adding some other University prize to my "Optimism." (*CLI*, 591)

In fact, Jack did get a first in Greats and then a first in English—giving him a triple first, a true rarity. The "Optimism" he refers to was a long essay he had written which had already garnered one award, the prestigious Chancellor's Prize, given annually to the best essay by an undergraduate.

What about Lewis's religious beliefs during this time? In the section of *Mere Christianity* titled "What Lies Behind the Law," Lewis outlines two basic views of the world.

> Ever since men were able to think they have been wondering what this universe really is and how it came to be there. And, very roughly, two views have been held. First, there is what is called the materialist view. People who take that view think that matter and space just happen to exist, and always have existed, nobody knows why; and that the matter behaving in certain fixed ways, has just happened, by a sort of fluke, to produce creatures like ourselves who are able to think. . . . The other view is the religious view. According to it, what is behind the universe is more like a mind than it is like anything else we know. That is to say, it is conscious, and has purposes, and prefers one thing to another. And on this view it made the universe partly for purposes we do not know, but partly, at any rate, in order to produce creatures like itself . . . to the extent of having minds. (21–22)

During the time he was an Oxford student, Jack worked very hard to assume a purely materialistic view, to put on what, in *Surprised by Joy*, he calls the New Look—a view of life made up of "no flirtations with any idea of the supernatural, no romantic delusions" (201). Lewis continues: "I decided I had done with all that. No more Avalon, no more Hesperides. I had . . . 'seen through' them. And I was never going to be taken in again" (204).

We can see Jack's New Look reflected in *The Last Battle*, a work published in 1956, a year after *Surprised by Joy*. In chapter 7, King Tirian invites the dwarfs to join the forces of the real Aslan. Griffle, speaking for the dwarfs, responds: "We've been taken in once and now you expect us to be taken in again the next minute. We've no more use for stories about Aslan" (82). Jack's New Look can also be found in Eustace's report of the much-changed Susan in chapter 12. There Eustace explains that when the topic of Narnia came up, Susan would respond, "Fancy your still thinking about all those funny games we used to play when we were children" (154). Alan Jacobs notes that during this time when Jack was formidably trying to put on his New Look, much like Susan he went "a long ways toward turning himself into someone who wouldn't even *read* books such as the Narnia stories" (102).

Jack's New Look required not merely complete disbelief in God but total disdain for such beliefs as well. In his essay for *Remembering C. S. Lewis: Recollections of Those Who Knew Him*, Leo Baker describes a conversation he had with Jack shortly after they both returned to Oxford from the war. When Baker asked Jack if he had been very frightened during his time in France, Jack replied, "All the time, but I never sank so low as to pray" (69).

And how did the feeling of Joy fit into Jack's New Look? Lewis writes that he now labeled it as mere aesthetic experience—something that had value but certainly not a value that could be called spiritual, because there was of course no such thing as spiritual. Not that this really mattered that much anyway, for during this time, as Lewis tells us in his autobiography, the experience of Joy "came very seldom and when it came it didn't amount to much" (205).

In the epigraph to chapter 13, Lewis compares his efforts to assume his New Look to Robinson Crusoe's attempt to build his great wall around his shelter. Here again we can find Jack's position reflected in the dwarves in *The Last Battle*. In chapter 13—titled "How the Dwarfs Refused to Be Taken In"—Aslan describes the wall of philosophical presuppositions they have surrounded themselves with: "They have chosen cunning instead of belief. Their prison is only in their own minds, yet they are in that prison; and so afraid of being taken in that they cannot be taken out" (169).

In the end, Robinson Crusoe's wall was not enough to guard him from outside attack. As we will see, Jack's New Look would also prove inadequate to shield him from his great adversary.

Oxford Don
and Reluctant Convert

(1 9 2 5 – 1 9 3 1)

You must picture me alone in that room in Magdalen,
night after night, feeling, whenever my mind lifted even
for a second from my work, the steady, unrelenting approach of Him whom I so earnestly desired not to meet.

—*Surprised by Joy*, chapter 14

Sweet Are the Uses of Adversity

The story of how Jack became an Oxford don begins with a
look backward.

Both Jack and Warnie inherited a defect in their thumb from
their father, making them unable to perform well in most sports.

This lack of aptitude in games was one of the reasons Jack found Malvern so difficult. Early in *Surprised by Joy*, Lewis explains: "The upper joint (that furthest from the nail) is visible, but it is a mere sham; we cannot bend it" (12). But in this adversity was something good, as Lewis also reports: "It was this that forced me to write." Of course, Lewis notes, when he was a boy frustrated by this misfortune, he had no idea of the "world of happiness" his defect was actually admitting him to. (We might say driving or guiding him to.)

Similarly, Lewis maintains that his two years at Wynyard, miserable though they were, also had a positive effect: "Life at a vile boarding school is in this way a good preparation for the Christian life, that it teaches one to live by hope. Even, in a sense, by faith" (36).

Lewis writes that as the end of his undergraduate days began to grow closer, the problem of finding a university teaching post afterward began to loom not only larger but also grimmer. In fact, the problem proved too large and too grim, at least initially, for when Jack finished with his two firsts in Mods and Greats and received his BA in 1922, he was unable to secure any job in philosophy, the field he was now trained in.

Warnie tells us in his memoir that even for a scholar of his brother's ability and achievement, it was neither a swift nor an easy matter to obtain an academic post. He describes the difficult process Jack went through in launching his academic career.

> Immediately after taking Greats, he sat for a Fellowship by Examination at Magdalen: before this he had looked into the possibility of a classical lectureship at Reading: later on, he applied for Fellowships at Trinity and St. John's. For all these posts, Jack saw other men chosen; and there were times during this period of uncertainty when he tended towards despair of any academic or literary success. (31)

With no job in philosophy—a fact which certainly must have seemed like another great adversity at the time—Jack decided, as noted previously, to spend the next year getting a degree in English.

In the English School, Jack met and quickly became friends with a fellow student named Nevill Coghill, who was not only the best-informed and most intelligent student in their class but also a thoroughgoing supernaturalist and a Christian.

An entry from Lewis's diary at the time records one of their typical hammer-and-tongs discussions.

> Coghill did most of the talking, except when contradicted by me. He said that Mozart had remained like a boy of six all his life. I said nothing could be more delightful: he replied (and quite right) that he could imagine many things more delightful. . . . He said that Blake was really inspired: I was beginning to say "In a sense—" when he said "In the same sense as Joan of Arc." I said, "I agree. In exactly the same sense. But we may mean different things." He: "If you are a materialist." (190)

Studying English literature brought Jack into contact with not only the Christian influence of Coghill, someone who could certainly hold his own in their lively debates, but another factor which threatened his naturalistic outlook. "All the books were beginning to turn against me," Lewis reports (213).

In this delightful passage from *Surprised by Joy*, Lewis recounts his feelings about the Christian authors he encountered at this time when he was desperately trying to remain a nonbeliever:

> George MacDonald had done more to me than any other writer; of course it was a pity he had that bee in his bonnet about Christianity. He was good *in spite of it*. Chesterton had more sense than all the other moderns put together; bating, of course, his Christianity. Johnson was one of the few authors whom I felt

I could trust utterly; curiously enough, he had the same kink.
Spenser and Milton by a strange coincidence had it too. . . .
But the most alarming of all was George Herbert. Here was a
man who seemed to me to excel all the authors I had ever read
in conveying the very quality of life as we actually live it from
moment to moment; but the wretched fellow, instead of doing
it all directly, insisted on mediating it through what I would still
have called "the Christian mythology." (213–14)

Lewis concludes that he must have been as blind as a bat
not to have seen the contradiction between his philosophical
worldview and his actual experience as a reader.

And what about those authors whose worldview aligned with
Jack's New Look—writers he should have embraced, such as
George Bernard Shaw, H. G. Wells, and John Stuart Mill? Lewis
comments that he found them entertaining but too simple and
lacking in depth.

In looking back at this time in his life, Lewis explains that
the normal step would have been to look more closely into the
claims of the Christian writers to see whether they were, after
all, wrong. But he did not take this step. Somehow Jack thought
he could explain their superiority without ever considering the
hypothesis that they were actually right.

But how was Jack's inability to obtain a position in philosophy a *sweet* adversity—an event Sayer refers to as a fortunate
failure? Because Jack could not get a philosophy position, he
went back for a degree in English. Then after a year with an
interim post, he was selected to be a fellow of Magdalen College (pronounced, as it has been for centuries, as *maudlin*) in
English language and literature. He would remain in English
for the rest of his career. This shift from philosophy to English
turned out not merely to suit Jack; it was vital to the shape of
the rest of his life. Had he gotten the post in philosophy he so
desperately desired immediately after finishing Greats in 1922,

he arguably would never have written the celebrated works he is now known for.

Here we must turn to two letters Jack wrote to Albert.

In the first, dated May 26, 1925, Jack—having just received the news of his appointment at Magdalen—expresses his gratitude for his father's financial support over the long, at times arduous, period that lasted from 1919 to 1925.

> First let me thank you from the bottom of my heart for the generous support, extended over six years, which alone has enabled me to hang on till this. In the long course I have seen men at least my equals in ability and qualifications fall out for the lack of it. . . . You have waited, not only without complaint but full of encouragement, while chance after chance slipped away and when the goal receded furthest from sight. Thank you again and again. (*CLI*, 642)

Even more touching is Albert's diary entry for May 20, 1925, when he first received Jack's telegraph conveying the good news: "I went up to his room and burst into tears of joy. I knelt down and thanked God with a full heart. My prayers had been heard and answered" (*LP*, 8:290).

In the second letter, written just three months later, Jack can already see that the move from philosophy to English, initially taken out of necessity, was truly for the best. He writes to Albert: "I am rather glad of the change. I have come to think that if I had the mind, I have not the brain and nerves for a life of pure philosophy. A continued search among the abstract roots of things, a perpetual questioning of all that plain men take for granted . . . is this the best life for temperaments such as ours?" (*CLI*, 648).

A. N. Wilson—who at the time he wrote his biography on Lewis did not share Lewis's faith and so in many ways saw the world quite differently—rightly points out that without Jack's pivotal shift to English, the story which followed might have been very different.

> Rich as his imagination was, it had not yet seen its truest modes of expression; brilliantly workable as his mind was, he had not yet discovered . . . the precise nature of what he was good *at*. . . . Without [the change to English], Lewis would not have been the man he became. . . . Classical Mods had confirmed his knowledge of and love for the great texts of Rome and Greece which were always to form so large a part of the furniture of Lewis's mind. Greats had sharpened his wits to the point where he thought not only that he was a philosopher, but that life and its problems could be adequately explained by purely cerebral means. English was to restore to him with inescapable force the message which he had been hearing . . . ever since he became addicted to reading as a small child in Northern Ireland. This was the knowledge that human life is best understood by the exercise of not only the wit, but also of the imagination. (75–77)

In Shakespeare's *As You Like It*, the Duke, who years earlier was deposed and exiled by his villainous brother, describes the truth he has come to see.

> Sweet are the uses of adversity,
> Which, like the toad, ugly and venomous,
> Wears yet a precious jewel in his head. (2.1.12–14)

Just as the ugly toad, which, legend reports, had a precious jewel with healing qualities embedded in its temple, Jack's own unpleasant, adverse circumstances also contained a precious gem hidden among them. Had there been an immediate opening in philosophy, Jack would never have gone into English and might never have written his fictional works such as *The Screwtape Letters* and the Chronicles of Narnia. But had he gone into English first, he would have lacked the training that enabled him to write such apologetic works such as *Miracles*, *The Problem of Pain*, and *Mere Christianity*.

Jack was formally admitted as an English fellow at Magdalen on June 25, 1925. In yet one more fortunate turn, one of the reasons he was hired was his ability to tutor in both English and philosophy. Jack was twenty-six.

"It is a formidable ceremony," he wrote to his father, "and not entirely to my taste" (*CLI*, 647). Being one of the largest colleges at Oxford, Magdalen had a sizable faculty. As part of the admissions ritual, Jack was required to stand in front of them all while the college vice president addressed him for five minutes in Latin. At the end of this exhortation, Jack, as required, responded *Do fidem*, which means "I swear." Then he was told, in English, to kneel on a red cushion which had been specially provided for the event. That done, the vice president took Jack by the hand and raised him to his feet with the words "I wish you joy." Jack tripped a little on his gown while rising, but he thought that at least the ceremony was over. Instead, he was sent around the room, where each of his fellow dons shook his hand and repeated the same phrase.

"I wish you joy."

"I wish you joy."

"I wish you joy."

What Jack did not foresee at the time—could not have foreseen—was how this wish was soon to come true.

"My external surroundings are beautiful beyond expectation," Jack wrote his father on October 21, 1925, from his new rooms at Magdalen (*CLI*, 650). He had a big sitting room which looked north over the college's deer park. It was here that he would write, prepare lectures, and hold student tutorials for the next thirty years. He had a smaller room which served as his bedroom that looked south across the broad, manicured lawn to the college's main buildings. Magdalen—the College of

St. Mary Magdalen—was founded in 1458. Its famous tower was completed in 1503. Jack's rooms were located in the college's New Building (or New Buildings, as the structure is sometimes called), so named following completion around 1733.

George Sayer, who as a student at Magdalen and one of Lewis's pupils would have spent many hours in tutorials in his rooms, offers this summary of Jack's new situation:

> At Magdalen he was looked after by a scout, a manservant whose duties included waking him up in the morning; bringing hot water for washing and shaving, for the rooms in New Buildings were without modern conveniences; clearing out the grates and lighting fires in one or both sitting rooms (there was no central heating); making the bed; and cleaning and tidying the rooms. In many other colleges, the scout would have also brought breakfast and lunch, but this was not the custom at Magdalen. . . . On all ordinary occasions, the fellows of the college ate in the dining room of the Senior Common Room, or for dinner, in hall. . . . Jack liked to eat breakfast early, because he would then have more time to complete his daily work. He arrived at eight or, when he had become a Christian, at a quarter past eight, after the fifteen-minute service in the college chapel. (187)

Lewis would later provide this answer to an American correspondent's question of what exactly an Oxford don does (his final statement about standing in queues, or lines, refers to the rationing in Britain after the war): "Like a woman, his work is never done. Taking 'tutorial' occupies the best part of his day, i.e., pupils come in pairs, read essays to him, then follows criticism, discussion, etc. Then he gives public lectures in his own subject; takes his share in the business of managing the College; prepares his lectures and writes books; and in his spare time stands in queues" (CLII, 855).

And so in the fall of 1925 we find Jack moved into his rooms at Magdalen to begin a thirty-year routine that would in many ways remain unchanged until 1955, when he would take up residence at Magdalene College, Cambridge (also pronounced like *maudlin* but spelled with an *e* at the end), after accepting the position of professor of medieval and Renaissance English literature. He would be at Cambridge until he resigned his position there in August 1963, just a few months before his death.

The New Look Crumbles and Jack Moves to Idealism

In *The Most Reluctant Convert*, David Downing offers this insight about the critical role Jack's atheism played in his later becoming such an effective Christian writer:

> A careful look at Lewis's early years reveals that he did not become an effective defender of the faith *despite* the fact that he spent so many years as an unbeliever. Rather, his Christian books are compelling precisely *because* he spent so many years as an unbeliever. He understood atheism. . . . He weighed all these worldviews himself, and eventually found them wanting. (15)

Here, in examining Lewis's journey of faith, we must briefly turn back to his days as an Oxford undergraduate—to the time when he tried very hard to fully embrace his New Look, the belief that the only reality is the universe as revealed by the senses. Like many of his fellow students, Jack took the position that what we can see, smell, touch, hear, or taste—on our own or aided by scientific instruments—is all there is. Gradually, through his own sometimes painful personal experience, he came to see the inconsistencies in this position.

As his undergrad days were drawing to a close, Lewis tells us in his autobiography, a "really dreadful thing" happened (205). Suddenly Jack's two best friends, Owen Barfield and Cecil Harwood, deserted the naturalistic position they had all proudly and defiantly held previously and became ardent believers in the supernatural, in a world beyond the physical world. Barfield and Harwood did not become Christians; they became followers of a religious system called anthroposophy, which at the time had a number of adherents among European intellectuals. Lewis reports that he was shocked by their change, claiming that everything he had labored so hard to expel from his own life seemed to have abruptly flared up and met him in his best friends.

Jack's two closest friends now embraced all that the New Look had been designed to exclude. Jack's main opposition to their belief in gods, spirits, and the afterlife was that it all was so, well, *medieval*. Lewis reports that Barfield was never able to convince him to be an anthroposophist, but Barfield quickly demolished the "chronological snobbery" which Jack was guilty of—the assumption that "whatever has gone out of date is on that account discredited" (207).

Losing this bias against old beliefs would be an essential step in Jack's conversion.

We find Lewis's most potent description of chronological snobbery in *The Screwtape Letters*. In the opening letter, Screwtape tells Wormwood that he needs to keep his patient thinking in terms not of whether something is true or false but of whether it is "outworn" or "contemporary" (1). "Don't waste time trying to make him think that materialism is *true!*" Screwtape advises. Instead Wormwood is to get him to think that it is "strong or stark or courageous"—that it is "the philosophy of the future" (2).

Screwtape revisits this topic later in discussing the "Historical Point of View," another term Lewis uses for chronological snobbery. In this devilishly delightful passage, Screwtape explains how this viewpoint works.

> The Historical Point of View, put briefly, means that when a learned man is presented with any statement in an ancient author, the one question he never asks is whether it is true. He asks

who influenced the ancient writer, and how far the statement is consistent with what he said in other books, and what phase in the writer's development, or in the general history of thought it illustrates, and how it affected later writers, and how often it has been misunderstood (specially by the learned man's own colleagues) and what the general course of criticism on it has been for the last ten years, and what is the "present state of the question." To regard the ancient writer as a possible source of knowledge—to anticipate that what he said could possibly modify your thoughts or your behavior—this would be rejected as unutterably simple-minded. (150–51)

Lewis was able to provide such a penetrating critique of chronological snobbery because he himself was guilty of it in his earlier years.

The one question he never asks is whether it is true. When Jack argued that Barfield's belief in the supernatural was medieval, Barfield rightly pointed out that even if that label applied, this fact alone did not mean his belief was false.

If the Historical Point of View is not an answer to a position held in the past but merely a statement of prejudice, in *Surprised by Joy* Lewis outlines what a valid argument against something which has gone out of date would look like, perhaps here giving words to what Barfield said to him: "You must find why it went out of date. Was it ever refuted (and if so by whom, where, and how conclusively) or did it merely die away as fashions do? If the latter, this tells us nothing about its truth or falsehood" (207–8).

With his chronological snobbery pointed out and its defect made plain, Jack was now ready to consider naturalism and supernaturalism on their own merits rather than simply to dismiss supernaturalism as being out of date. And when he did consider the two positions, he found naturalism to be inconsistent in several ways.

In examining his own naturalism—he also calls it realism, popular realism, or materialism—Lewis tells us that he encountered three problems.

The first had to do with reason. Jack was unable to abandon the claim that abstract thought done rigorously and logically would lead to truth. This concept was something the Great Knock had knocked into Jack so thoroughly that we could say he was infused or permeated with it. At the same time, Jack came to the conclusion that naturalism could not support this belief.

Lewis titles the second chapter of *Miracles* "The Cardinal Difficulty of Naturalism," and this difficulty he refers to is the problem that if our thoughts are merely the product of random accidents, then there is no reason to trust them. Lewis argues here that naturalism "discredits our processes of reasoning or at least reduces their credit to such a humble level that it can no longer support Naturalism itself" (15).

In his essay "Is Theology Poetry?" Lewis outlines this first problem he had with materialism.

> Long before I believed theology to be true, I had already decided that the popular scientific picture at any rate was false. One absolutely central inconsistency ruins it. The whole picture professes to depend on inferences from observed facts. Unless inference is valid, the whole picture disappears. . . . Unless Reason is an absolute, all is in ruins. Yet those who ask me to believe this world picture also ask me to believe that Reason is simply the unforeseen and unintended by-product of mindless matter at one stage of its endless and aimless becoming. Here is flat contradiction. They ask me at the same moment to accept a conclusion and to discredit the only testimony on which that conclusion can be based. The difficulty is to me a fatal one. (135)

Jack's second problem with naturalism had to do with morality or ethics. Jack was unable to abandon the idea that certain moral judgments could be labeled as valid, or at least as more valid than certain others—and with Barfield's help, he came to the conclusion that naturalism could not support this belief. In *Mere Christianity*, Lewis presents the problem this way:

> The moment you say that one set of moral ideas can be better than another, you are, in fact, measuring them both by a standard, saying that one of them conforms to that standard more nearly than the other. But the standard that measures two things is something different from either. You are, in fact, comparing them both with some Real Morality, admitting that there is such a thing as a Real Right, independent of what people think. (13)

But where did this "Real Morality" come from in a universe where humankind was just the product of random accident? This was Jack's second problem with naturalism.

The third problem had to do with aesthetics. Jack was unable to abandon the idea that our experience of the beautiful is more than merely an encounter with something pleasing to the senses. Once again, he found naturalism was unable to sustain this position. As Lewis states in chapter 11 of *Surprised by Joy*, materialism, if followed to its logical conclusion, meant that "one had to look out on a meaningless dance of atoms" and to realize that "all the apparent beauty was a subjective phosphorescence, and to relegate everything one valued to the world of mirage" (172–73). In his essay "De Futilitate," he argues, "There is no reason why our reaction to a beautiful landscape should not be the response, however humanly blurred and partial, to something that is really there" (71).

Lewis reports in his autobiography that he found he could no more disbelieve or abandon these three positions on reason, ethics, and aesthetics—or, we might say, on truth, goodness, and beauty—than he could scratch his ear with his big toe. "I was therefore compelled to give up Realism," he concludes (209).

And so Jack became a philosophical idealist, a position not talked about much today but quite popular at Oxford at the time. And though he did not know it, this idealism was not going to be a final destination but only the next stop on his journey.

Idealism Soon Crumbles and Jack Moves to an Impersonal Theism

When Jack abandoned realism, the belief that the physical world is all there is, and embraced idealism, the belief that there was some sort of Absolute that transcended the physical world, things started off well, *initially*. "This was a religion that cost nothing," Lewis writes in *Surprised by Joy*. "We could talk religiously about the Absolute: but there was no danger of Its doing anything about us" (210).

Lewis notes the influence of three idealists—the English Hegelians—T. H. Green, F. H. Bradley, and Bernard Bosanquet. Perhaps a closer look at just one of them will be sufficient to indicate the general position taken by idealist thinkers at the time. In *The Most Reluctant Convert*, David Downing offers this summary of the thesis in Bradley's influential work *Appearance and Reality*:

> Bradley envisioned an all-embracing Absolute in which the contradictions and illusions of the sensory world are transcended and resolved. This Absolute should not be confused with the God of religion, because it is not a Person apart from the universe; rather it is immanent in the universe, transforming the physical into the metaphysical. Just as each human body has a "soul," the Absolute is the "soul" of the cosmos. (128)

Looking back at the idealism which he embraced at this time, Lewis writes in his autobiography that it was astonishing that he could view this position as something distinct from theism and concludes: "I suspect there was some willful blindness" (209).

In addition to his own willful blindness, Jack had help from the idealist philosophers, who provided him with a number of useful "blankets, insulators, and insurances" which allowed him to get all the "conveniences" of theism without having to actually believe in God.

Writing in 1943 in the afterword to the third edition of *The Pilgrim's Regress*, Lewis traces his faith journey this way: "On the intellectual side my own progress had been from 'popular realism' to Philosophical Idealism; from Idealism to Pantheism; from Pantheism to Theism; and from Theism to Christianity" (200). These stages are perhaps worth unpacking a bit. Jack's idealism held that there was a vague Absolute—but its nature, location, and other attributes were left largely undefined. Jack's pantheism then saw this Absolute as immanent in and part of the universe. Finally, his theism placed this Absolute above and apart from the physical universe. There were two stages to Jack's theism, as he first came to believe in an impersonal Spirit and then later in a personal God. After his move to theism, Jack still had a final move to Christianity.

Lewis goes on to say in the afterword that while he believes his path to belief to be a very natural road, at the same time he confesses that he had come to see his own particular sequence of steps to faith as a road very rarely trodden. In fact, very few Christians today have followed Lewis's intellectual path. One reason for this, Lewis goes on to note, is that idealism soon ceased to have the appeal it had when he was one of its adherents. "The dynasty of Green, Bradley, and Bosanquet fell," Lewis observes, "and the world inhabited by philosophical students of my own generation became as alien to our successors as if not years but centuries had intervened" (200).

Lewis concludes that in looking back on *The Pilgrim's Regress* ten years after its release, he finds in it a good deal of needless obscurity. Had he known his faith journey was so unfamiliar to the vast majority of his readers, he admits that he would have tried to describe it with more consideration for their difficulties. "I committed the same sort of blunder as one who should narrate his travels through the Gobi Desert on the assumption that this route was as familiar to the British public as the line from Euston to Crewe," Lewis confesses (200).

A decade later, writing of this same journey from idealism to theism in *Surprised by Joy*, Lewis again at times becomes obscure and, to use his own comparison, may leave some readers feeling like they have been abandoned in the Gobi. Biographer Alan Jacobs throws up his hands at this point in Lewis's narrative, asking, "But how, then, did he get from his vague Hegelian Absolute Spirit to a personal God?" His conclusion is that Lewis's account is "hard to understand" (129).

The progression in Lewis's faith journey from idealism to theism as described in his autobiography *is* hard to understand—particularly when looked at in its individual parts. But it is easier to follow when viewed as a whole—if we look at how each of these steps was connected to Joy, the central story of Lewis's life, and how Joy now for the very first time *became integrated into his worldview.*

Lewis titles chapter 14 of *Surprised by Joy* "Checkmate." There will be only one more chapter to follow. Five pages into chapter 14, Lewis tells us, "My Adversary began to make His final moves" (216).

Exactly how many of these final moves there were is hard to determine. Using phrases like "the first Move" and "the next Move"—each time, the word *move* is capitalized, presumably to suggest its divine origin—Lewis goes on to describe four specific steps. But along with these, he also mentions several other events that played a role in his acceptance of theism. Did Lewis consider these other events as moves made by his adversary? It's impossible to say.

Even the exact dates for this transition are hard to pinpoint. Jack's final step to fully embrace theism—the night when he finally accepted that God was God—took place during Trinity term (which runs from April through June) of 1929. We know this because Lewis tells us so in the last paragraph of chapter 14. (That said, evidence from an earlier manuscript version of Surprised by Joy suggests that this year may have been 1930 rather than 1929. So this may be another place—like the age he reports going off to school in 1911 and the month he reports having discovered *Phantastes*—where Lewis is slightly off.)

When did this step begin? Just before launching into his account of these final moves, Lewis mentions two events which can be dated. First, he mentions his father's death—simply to note it and claim that it does not come into the story which he is telling. The problem is that Albert's death took place on September 25, 1929, three months *after* the end of Trinity term—making it unclear what this date has to do with the checkmate Jack undergoes. After mentioning his father's death, Lewis then goes backward to mention his election as a fellow at Magdalen in 1925, possibly suggesting this as a starting date. So perhaps we might bookend his journey from idealism to personal theism with the years 1925 and 1929.

On May 26, 1926, seven months after moving into his rooms in the New Building, Jack wrote in his diary: "I took my walk over the fields to the row of firs on the way to Forest Hill, and sat down at the foot of one where there was a pleasant breeze. The place is smothered in daisies and buttercups and hedged with hawthorn. I thought a little—all my ideas are in a crumbling state at present" (401). During this time, each step in Lewis's spiritual journey will be marked by a crumbling of one stage, that door closing, and a door to the next stage opening.

Lewis reports that his adversary's first move came because he reread *Hippolytus* by Euripides, and this triggered the return of

Joy which had been long absent. How did Jack happen to pick up this particular text at this particular time? Besides calling this a *move* on the part of his adversary, Lewis makes a point to tell us in his autobiography that he was suddenly "impelled" to reread this work (217). What drove him to reread this work we are not told. It was not something he *needed* to read at the time. Lewis states that *Hippolytus* was "certainly no business of mine at the moment," further suggesting that in both the rereading and the Joy that accompanied it, his adversary was at work.

Lewis reports that in one moment all the play's imagery of the world's end rose before him, presumably a reference to this moving passage:

> Oh God, bring me to the end of the seas
> To the Hesperides, sisters of evening,
> Who sing alone in their islands
> Where the golden apples grow,
> And the Lord of Oceans guards the way
> From all who would sail
> Into their night-blue harbors—
> Let me escape to the rim of the world
> Where the tremendous firmament meets
> The earth, and Atlas holds the universe
> In his palms.
> For there, in the palace of Zeus,
> Wells of ambrosia pour through the chambers,
> While the sacred earth lavishes life
> And Time adds his years
> Only to heaven's happiness. (98)

Lewis says that at once he was transported to the land of longing, where his heart was both broken and exalted as it had not been since his days at Great Bookham with the Kirkpatricks. Finally the long inhibition was over. The dry desert where Joy was forbidden by the realism of the New Look was suddenly behind him, never to be returned to.

Bring me to the end of the seas. Let me escape to the rim of the world where the tremendous firmament meets the earth. Lewis would never forget the deep longing the imagery in these lines evoked. Years later, in the climactic final chapter of *The Voyage of the Dawn Treader*, he would create his own equally moving version of the world's end. Modern readers, who find it difficult to share Jack's experience of Joy from reading *Hippolytus*, often find Reepicheep's longing for Aslan's Country, where sky and water meet, to be one of the most beautiful and moving elements in the entire Narnia series.

If the first step in Jack's embrace of theism was the return of Joy to his life, the second step was also related to Joy. In what Lewis calls the next move by his adversary, we are offered a convoluted, four-page discussion of the effect that Samuel Alexander's distinction between *enjoyment* and *contemplation* had on his conception of Joy. (These two terms are defined by Alexander in *Space, Time, and Deity* in a highly technical way that has nothing to do with either pleasure or the contemplative life.)

Whether it is possible to fully make sense of the threefold division Lewis proposes in this part of *Surprised by Joy* between the unconscious, the enjoyed, and the contemplated is debatable. What is clear is that because of reading *Space, Time, and Deity*, Jack came to see that his experience of Joy was really just a footprint of something greater, not the wave but the imprint of the wave on the sand, a pointer to something else.

Noted Lewis scholar Clyde Kilby offers this explanation of what Jack came to understand from reading Alexander's work:

> A thought is not simply a thing inside one's own head and isolated from its object. Introspection can only find what is left behind and cannot operate while the original thought exists. It is a terrible error to mistake the track left behind for the thing

itself. Immediately Lewis knew he was looking in the wrong place to find the Joy he had long sought. . . . He had always been wrong in thinking that he desired Joy itself. (18–19)

Lewis tells us that it was as if Joy had explained to him, *I myself am your want of something outside yourself.* This realization, Lewis writes, brought him into the "region of awe," because at this point he came to understand that his experience of Joy was evidence, in his case irrefutable evidence, of something supernatural beyond himself—something which he could, in his words, have "commerce" with (221).

If Joy was the footprint, Jack suddenly came to understand there must be a foot.

Later, this *something* supernatural would become *someone.* Later, Jack would ask, *who* is the desired? At this point he stopped at, *what* is it? Still, even this was overpowering. In trying to describe what happened to him at this step of realization, Lewis simply states that awe overtook him. And perhaps this awe provides a partial explanation for Alan Jacobs's claim that this step is too hard to understand. Anytime we are taken into this region of awe in someone else's story, obscurity and inscrutability must of necessity set in.

This second move, his coming to see that Joy was only a footprint of something else, Lewis describes as the equivalent of losing his last remaining bishop. The third move initially seemed harmless to Jack, like losing a pawn. But in looking back, this was the kind of loss of a pawn which leads in a few moves to a checkmate. Lewis writes that this third move consisted "merely" in linking his new realization about Joy with his philosophical idealism (222).

Jack's thinking as an idealist ran something like this: All human creatures have the root of their existence in the Absolute. Because of this, we yearn to be reunited with this Absolute. For Jack this meant—well, it is hard to say exactly what this meant.

Here we must turn to Lewis's own explanation in *Surprised by Joy*, and even with it readers may still find this move hard to follow. Lewis writes the following about the link between Joy and his conception of the Absolute:

> We mortals, seen as the sciences see us and as we commonly see one another, are mere "appearance." But appearances of the Absolute. . . . That is why we experience Joy: we yearn, rightly, for the unity which we can never reach except by ceasing to be the separate phenomenal beings called "we." Joy was not a deception. Its visitations were rather the moments of clearest consciousness we had, when we became aware of our fragmentary and phantasmal nature and ached for that impossible reunion which would annihilate us or that self-contradictory waking which would reveal, not that we had had, but that we *were*, a dream. (221–22)

Lewis comments that this train of thought was both intellectually and emotionally satisfying to him. For his readers, it may serve simply as a help in understanding why idealism as a philosophical movement died out so quickly.

What is clear from this third move is that the two great sources of meaning in Jack's life—his experience of Joy and his philosophical perspective—were now connected. At the time, this connection did not seem all that important to Lewis. Soon, it would prove critical.

A defining attribute of Jack's personality was what might be called his consistency of thought. The fourth move by his adversary came about because of this deep need for intellectual integrity which characterized Jack.

One reason Jack had been chosen for the fellowship at Magdalen was his ability to teach both English and philosophy, and early on he tutored some students who were reading philosophy—though in his autobiography he claims to have done it rather poorly. His role as a tutor, as he saw it, was to make things clear. The problem, Lewis reports, was that the idealistic Absolute was a concept which could not be made clear. Jack found he could not in good conscience go on pretending that Hegel's Absolute—though quite in fashion—was really more than a mystifying add-on and a way of obscuring simple theism.

In the end, Jack found that he needed a position of his own to serve as a basis for critiquing his pupils' essays and had to choose between an Absolute that was "nobody-knows-what" and something that was a kind of superhuman mind and therefore a person (222). Jack, as a tutor trying to make things clear, was driven to the latter. He made a point in telling his students that his position did *not* embrace the God of popular religion. No, his was a *philosophical* God. But no matter what he called this person, Lewis reports that the fox had been chased from the Hegelian wood.

And so Jack ceased to be an idealist who believed in a vague Absolute and became a theist who believed in a philosophical God, the next step on his road to faith.

From Impersonal Theism to a Personal God

Halfway through Lewis's account of how he was checkmated by his adversary, we find this wonderful description of how, after becoming what we might call a reluctant theist, he would attempt to articulate his highly nuanced beliefs about the remote and unapproachable God he now admitted must exist.

> There was, I explained, no possibility of being in a personal relation with Him. For I thought He projected us as a dramatist projects his characters, and I could no more "meet" Him, than Hamlet could meet Shakespeare. I didn't call Him "God" either; I called Him "Spirit." One fights for one's remaining comforts. (223)

And so readers say a fond farewell to Jack's Hegelian idealism and move on to a stage which they can perhaps—except for the "He projected us as a dramatist projects his characters" part—much more readily understand and perhaps identify with: the belief in an impersonal God who is off somewhere far away and does not interfere with humans or with anything.

I didn't call Him "God." On January 18, 1927, Jack wrote in his diary, "All the time (with me) there's the danger of falling back into most childish superstitions" (432). Presumably, by "childish superstitions" he is referring to belief in God and Christianity, beliefs which in his mind were still associated with the nursery and the kind of thing a person should outgrow.

One fights for one's remaining comforts. Why would Jack find it a comfort for God to remain merely an impersonal Spirit? Wouldn't the idea of a loving Father in heaven be more comforting? Near the end of chapter 14, Lewis reminds us that above all things in life he wanted not to be interfered with, to be able to call his soul his own. At this point Jack is most like his character Jane Studdock from *That Hideous Strength*, who resolves not to be drawn in. "To avoid entanglements and interferences had long been one of her principles," Lewis's narrator explains (71).

It is at this stage in Lewis's faith journey that the epigraph he chose for chapter 14 becomes relevant. The sentence, italicized below, is from a passage in George MacDonald's *Unspoken Sermons*. The passage describes Lewis's position at the time. It could be said to describe everyone's position before submitting to God's will.

For the one principle of hell is—"I am my own." I am my own king and my own subject. I am the center from which go out my thoughts; I am the object and end of my thoughts; back upon me as the alpha and omega of life, my thoughts return. My own glory is, and ought to be, my chief care; my ambition, to gather the regards of men to the one center, myself. My pleasure is my pleasure. My kingdom is—as many as I can bring to acknowledge my greatness over them. My judgment is the faultless rule of things. My right is—what I desire. (332)

After telling us he was like a fox driven from Hegelian wood, Lewis reports that nearly everyone and everything—all the great writers, all his close friends, and even Joy itself—seemed to be in the pack chasing him from his idealism to his final belief in a personal God. Good books and good friends were critical in Lewis's conversion. And the next book to play a major role was by an author he had discovered six years before in a hospital on the coast of France while recuperating from trench fever.

"You will remember," Lewis self-mockingly tells us in *Surprised by Joy*, "that I already thought Chesterton the most sensible man alive 'apart from his Christianity'" (223). Earlier Lewis had been impressed by a book of Chesterton's essays. Now Chesterton's *The Everlasting Man* would lay out for Jack the "whole Christian outline of history" in a form that made sense. Chesterton's work was published in 1925, to some extent as a rebuttal of H. G. Wells's *Outline of History* which had been published five years earlier.

We should note how far Jack has come since he declared to Arthur Greeves ten years earlier, in 1916: "I believe in no religion. There is absolutely no proof for any of them, and from a philosophical standpoint Christianity is not even the best" (*CLI*, 230–31). Now the Christian outline of history made more sense to Jack than its secular counterpart. Lewis observes that after reading *The Everlasting Man* he was brought to the nonsensical position of believing that Christianity itself was very sensible *apart from its Christianity*.

"Somehow I contrived not to be too badly shaken," he states (223).

But Jack's former position about the inadequacy of the Christian version of history *had* been shaken, badly shaken. Someone was closing in on Jack, though he did not realize it. Not yet.

The impact which Chesterton's book had cannot be over-stated. In 1962, just a year before his death, Lewis was asked by the *Christian Century* which books had been the most influential in his thinking. Of the thousands and thousands he had read over the course of his life, Jack picked just ten. The first two on the list were *Phantastes* and *The Everlasting Man*.

In the diary entry for April 27, 1926, Lewis notes that T. D. Weldon, one of his colleagues who tutored philosophy at Magdalen, stopped by his rooms for a chat that went late into the night. "We somehow got on the historical truth of the Gospels," Lewis records (379). This conversation appears to be the one Lewis refers to in *Surprised by Joy* where he describes a visit from a militant skeptic who remarked, "All that stuff of Frazer's about the Dying God. Rum thing. It almost looks as if it had really happened once" (223–24). To understand the impact this comment had on him, Lewis says that we must know that the speaker was the hardest of hardboiled cynics, "the toughest of the toughs." If this atheist of atheists was not safe, what did this say about Lewis's own position?

Jack's late-night conversation with Weldon, and Weldon's startling statement about the strong case for the historicity of the Gospels, is one of the better-known incidents in *Surprised by Joy*. Coming as it did in 1926, the conversation did *not* at this point lead to Jack's acceptance of Christianity, which did not happen until five years later, in 1931. So why does Lewis include this episode here among the steps which led him to a belief in a personal God? This admission coming from this specific person forced Jack to reexamine his position on what he thought was and was not possible.

Later Lewis would use his fiction in this very same way. Through story he sought to break down readers' preconceived notions and open them to new possibilities. Philip Yancey has pointed out this capacity of Lewis's fiction to dismantle "barriers to faith" plank by plank and introduce readers to "another way of seeing" (94). Because of this ability, Stephen Smith has referred to Lewis's fictional works, such as the Chronicles of Narnia, as "pre-apologetics" (168), works that serve to make those who have been closed to the gospel message more predisposed to hear it.

Weldon's comment, Chesterton's compelling outline of history, and Jack's grudging acceptance of the existence of at least a philosophical God—these all came together, of all times and places, as Jack was riding home on the bus. Colin Duriez offers this dramatized rendition of this key moment in Lewis's story.

Imagine an early summer's day in the Trinity term of 1929, around lunchtime. The location is the upper deck of the Headington bus, starting its journey up the hill eastwards from the Oxford city center. A man sits there, about thirty, wearing a tweed jacket and baggy flannels, and a shabby hat on his head, with the brim turned down all around. He could be a young farmer, with his red complexion and thick-set form.

He looks out of the bus window, putting his cigarette to his lips and drawing its smoke into his lungs, apparently gazing over Headington Hill Park. The man is C. S. Lewis, and he is starting to grapple with a momentous decision. . . . Unprovoked by any particular event of the bus journey, Lewis suddenly feels presented with a fact about himself. . . . He senses that he has been shutting something out, holding something at bay. He would describe it later as if wearing uncomfortable clothing—like a cumbersome suit of armor. . . . It is as if suddenly a door appears before him that he can push open, or leave shut. He chooses in an instant to go through the door. . . . As he acts, he is freer than ever before, yet the choice is demanded by his deepest nature. (45)

In his autobiography, Lewis writes that before the bus ride was finished, he had made the choice "to open, to unbuckle, to loosen the rein" (224). These are metaphors, surely, for the process—but ones which imply that he had been doing the opposite: that through an act of will he had been closed and buckled up against something he wanted to keep at bay; that he had previously chosen to keep a tight rein on where intellectual investigation might lead him rather than letting philosophical inquiry take him where it would.

I chose to open, to unbuckle, to loosen the rein. There would be more choices and further steps to take as Jack slowly came to admit that God was God and then to accept Christ, but it could be argued that this decision—this calm, dispassionate choice made on the top of a bus going up Headington Hill—was the hinge upon which his whole life would pivot. For at this moment he decided to be open to the truth no matter what direction that truth might go, to not hold anything or anyone at bay—not anymore. And once he gave free rein to truth, once he let go of the reins he had pulled in so tightly, Jack would find that truth would take him to only one place.

In *Surprised by Joy*, Lewis tells us that the decision on the bus top took place "before God closed in" (224). God would not close in on Jack without permission. On the bus ride up Headington Hill, permission was given.

Lewis writes that following his decision he felt like a frozen snowman at long last beginning to melt, slowly at first, then faster and faster—drip, drip and then trickle, trickle. Lewis admits that he rather disliked the feeling. But shouldn't letting go and unbuckling be an enjoyable feeling? Perhaps Jack did feel some relief in taking off the rigid suit of armor he had been wearing for so long—but if so, relief was not the dominant feeling.

Drip, drip, trickle, trickle. With Jack's protective shell now removed, we sense the torrent that is to come. Lewis says this decision on the bus top was all or nothing—and he chose all. To open the door and take off his armor "meant the incalculable" (224). It could be argued that right at or near the top of the list of things Jack feared was the incalculable. Now anything might happen; truly, anything.

And it did happen—not in a day or even a week but over the coming months and the next two years. Drip, drip, trickle, trickle, as the snowman continued to melt.

And God continued to close in.

God Closes In

The final steps of Lewis's acceptance of and submission to a personal God take on a character different from the previous ones. They are less gradual and more intense, less intellectual and more personal—less about actions Jack was taking and more about actions his adversary was taking. And this is as it should be, for, as Lewis tells us, each successive step was a step toward something more concrete, more imminent, more compulsive.

Earlier it was pointed out that one of Jack's defining characteristics was his need for consistency of thought, for intellectual integrity. Now, as Jack moved closer to a belief in God, he felt a growing need for consistency of behavior, an integration of belief and actions. This desire to not only talk the talk but also walk the walk was not something totally new for Jack. Readers may remember that as a young boy at Oldies, Jack for a time became an effective believer and in response began to pray seriously, read the Bible, and attempt to obey his conscience. It was also during this time that he began making the list of resolutions that he carried in his pocket. Now, two decades later, Jack's beliefs again demanded a response.

Another comment, this one made during an informal lunch in Jack's rooms at Magdalen, became a catalyst for this next step.

Jack was eating with his pupil Alan Griffiths and his friend Owen Barfield when the topic of philosophy came up. Griffiths would later become a Benedictine monk and take the name we find in Lewis's dedication of *Surprised by Joy*, Dom Bede Griffiths. When Jack happened to refer to philosophy as a subject, Barfield quickly objected that philosophy was not a *subject* to Plato but *a way*. Lewis writes, "The quiet but fervent agreement of Griffiths, and the quick glance of understanding between these two, revealed to me my own frivolity" (225).

Jack immediately saw that Barfield and Griffiths were right. His own position was frivolous. Jack recognized that philosophy could not be merely another abstract subject, merely something a person might major in or teach. In the next sentence from *Surprised by Joy*, we find Jack's response: "Enough had been thought, and said, and felt, and imagined. It was about time that something should be done" (225). Later, as a Christian believer, Jack would also see an undeniable need to put his beliefs into practice and, among other specific actions, would give away the majority of his book royalties to those in need and answer hundreds of letters seeking his advice. Now, as someone who believed in an increasingly personal God, what would this mean in his day-to-day living?

In *theory* there had always been an ethical component in Jack's idealism. Theoretically, Jack had believed that we as humans were supposed to remember our true nature and in doing so ought to "reascend or return into that Spirit which, in so far as we really were at all, we still were" (226), whatever that meant. Lewis writes that he came to the conclusion that although a belief in an impersonal, undefined Spirit can be talked about and even felt, it cannot be *lived*. But once you believed in a God who was more than a "philosophical theorem, cerebrally entertained," as Jack now did, a "wholly new situation developed" (227).

Back in 1920 Lewis had written to a friend, "In the course of my philosophy—on the existence of matter—I have had to postulate some sort of God as the least objectionable theory" (*CLI*, 509). Now, as Lewis tells us in *Surprised by Joy*, the dry, dusty bones of what he once viewed as a philosophical postulate stood up and became a living presence. And for the first time, Jack saw that the initiative for his encounter with the divine did not lie with him. To talk of man's search for God now seemed as naive and misguided as talking about the mouse's search for the cat. Jack began to feel the steady, unfaltering approach of a God he did not really want to meet.

There are many pictures of the stately New Building at Magdalen showing its cloistered walkway and the windows of the two floors located above it. The two windows marking Jack's rooms are easy to locate because they are on the second floor directly above the wisteria vine on the right as you face the building. And now we come to the most famous passage in all of *Surprised by Joy*.

> You must picture me alone in that room in Magdalen night after night, feeling, whenever my mind lifted even for a second from my work, the steady, unrelenting approach of Him whom I so earnestly desired not to meet. That which I greatly feared had at last come upon me. In the Trinity Term of 1929 I gave in, and admitted that God was God, and knelt and prayed: perhaps, that night, the most dejected and reluctant convert in all England. (228–29)

Lewis goes on to point out the divine humility—we might add, the divine compassion—which accepts such an unwilling and unenthusiastic convert. He contrasts his own story with that of the prodigal son whose homecoming was made on his own two feet. But perhaps Lewis is being too hard on himself here. The prodigal son was returning home to a father he had known all his life—though, in the end, he still underestimated his father's love by thinking that *maybe* if he were contrite enough his father might treat him as one of his servants. Unlike the prodigal, Jack gave in to a God he did not know, a God who might demand anything.

"For all I knew, the total rejection of what I called Joy might be one of the demands, might be the very first demand, He would make upon me," Lewis explains (230). Here Jack may seem uncharacteristically unthinking to some. Yes, he had not met this God before, but he knew those who had. This was the God of MacDonald, the God of Chesterton, the God of Herbert, the God of Tolkien, and the God of Coghill—men who had tasted the goodness of God and whose experience Jack could take at least some confidence in. We find a similar situation in *Prince Caspian*, when Trumpkin is terrified to meet Aslan, but not completely terrified, for he has the testimony of Peter, Susan, Edmund, and Lucy—friends who had met the great lion and knew him to be not only terrible but also good.

Lewis finishes the account of his checkmate with a quote from the parable of the great banquet found in Luke 14. He gives its Latin version, *compelle intrare* ("compel them to come in"), to point us to the historic practice of using force to coerce members of other faiths or nonorthodox sects to convert. Lewis comments that while Christ's words have been so abused down through history that they may cause us to shudder, God's compulsion is quite different from ours. When understood properly—as Jack now did understand them—the words *compelle intrare* "plumb the depths of Divine mercy" (229).

Lewis characterizes himself as someone who was brought in "kicking, struggling, resentful, and darting his eyes in every direction for a chance of escape" (229). We could say he was compelled, but this would be only part of the story. We must also keep in mind the wholly free decision Jack made earlier atop the double-decker bus when he was presented with the choice to open the door or keep it shut. There was no kicking or struggling then—only the perfectly free option of saying yes or no to something he had been keeping at bay and could have continued keeping at bay had he wanted to.

Let us return to Lewis's own words about that choice:

> I chose to open, to unbuckle, to loosen the rein. I say, "I chose," yet it did not really seem possible to do the opposite. . . . You could argue that I was not a free agent, but I am more inclined to think that this came nearer to being a perfectly free act than most that I have ever done. Necessity may not be the opposite of freedom. (224)

It did not really seem possible to do the opposite. This came nearer to being a perfectly free act than most that I have ever done. How can Lewis's seemingly divergent claims here be made compatible?

Perhaps they can't. In his *Confessions*, Augustine tells God, "You follow close behind the fugitive and recall us to yourself in ways we cannot understand" (75). In a letter dated August 3, 1953, Lewis initially claims, "Everyone looking back on *his own* conversion must feel—and I am sure the feeling is in some sense true—'It is not *I* who have done this'" (*CLIII*, 354–55). But then he goes on to insist, "The real inter-relation between God's omnipotence and Man's freedom is something we can't find out."

In *Letters to Malcolm*, Lewis writes about the relationship of God's will and our free will in this way:

> You will notice that Scripture just sails over the problem. "Work out your own salvation in fear and trembling"—pure Pelagianism. But why? "For it is God who worketh in you"—pure Augustinianism. It is presumably only our presuppositions that make this appear nonsensical. We profanely assume that divine

and human action exclude one another like the actions of two fellow-creatures so that "God did this" and "I did this" cannot both be true of the same act except in the sense that each contributed a share. (49–50)

This came nearer to being a perfectly free act than most that I have ever done. It did not really seem possible to do the opposite. In a scene from *The Silver Chair* where Jill finds herself alone and thirsty on a great mountain in Aslan's Country, Lewis perhaps shows us how these statements can be reconciled. When the great lion she meets there asks if she is thirsty, she tells him she is dying of thirst. And yet, out of fear of him, she dares not come closer and drink from the stream he is lying beside. When she tells the lion that since he will not move, she will have to go and look for another stream, he informs her, "There is no other stream" (23).

In the end, Jill chooses to go to the stream and drink. Similarly, we could say that rather than die of thirst Jack chose to drink from the only stream there was. In this sense Lewis includes both necessity and freedom in his decision. He ends chapter 14 of *Surprised by Joy* embracing the paradox: "His compulsion is our liberation" (229). In these final words we can hear echoes of John Donne, who declares in "Holy Sonnet XIV" that unless God enthralled him, he would never be free—and so asks God to batter his heart, words that resonate with Lewis's own story.

Possibly because Lewis was one himself, the story of the reluctant convert who resists at first but in the end comes the long way round to belief was one of his favorites. John from *The Pilgrim's Regress* is certainly one. Jane Studdock from *That Hideous Strength* has already been mentioned. In *Out of the Silent Planet*, Ransom is told by the great Oyarsa, "You have taken many vain troubles to avoid standing where you stand now" (121). In *Perelandra*, Lewis himself appears as a character whose greatest fear is being drawn in. In each of these characters, we can find a reflection of Lewis's own experience. But perhaps we see him best in Trumpkin's encounter with Aslan in *Prince Caspian*, mentioned earlier. All along, the skeptical dwarf has thought the idea of a great lion from across the sea to be "all bilge and beanstalks" (148).

Contemptuous of what he calls old wives' tales, Trumpkin will believe in only what he can see with his own eyes. The stout dwarf declares, "I have no use for magic lions which are talking lions and don't talk, and friendly lions though they don't do us any good, and whopping big lions though nobody can see them" (148). In the end, as they did Jack, events bring Trumpkin to an encounter with the One whom he most earnestly desired not to meet.

"And now, where is this little Dwarf . . . who doesn't believe in lions?" Aslan roars out and orders Trumpkin to approach (154). Aslan takes the terrified former skeptic in his mouth and gives him a great shake before setting him back on his feet and asking, "Son of Earth, shall we be friends?" (155). In the Trinity term of 1929, six months after his thirtieth birthday, Jack knelt and prayed, and took the first step in what would be a lifelong friendship.

Jack's Final Step to Belief in Christ: The Road to Whipsnade

The famous final paragraph of chapter 14 of *Surprised by Joy*, where Jack finally gives in and admits that God is God, is heavy with allusions to the New Testament. Lewis refers to the parable of the prodigal son, who at least came home on his own feet, and to the parable of the great banquet, with the master's command to compel them to come. In Lewis's statement "The hardness of God is kinder than the softness of men" (229), we hear echoes of 1 Corinthians 1:25, where St. Paul tells us that the foolishness of God is wiser than the wisdom of men and that the weakness of God is stronger than the strength of men. With these references, it is easy to see why someone who reads this paragraph in isolation might assume that this was the moment when Jack accepted Christ.

It wasn't.

Lewis makes this point clear in the opening sentence of chapter 15, where we are told that what the most dejected and reluctant convert in all England had converted to in Trinity term of 1929 was theism "pure and simple"—not Christianity (230). This final step would not come until two years later, in September 1931, and it would not come without further opposition on Jack's part. Lewis writes that his need to call his soul his own was again an obstacle to belief, creating a resistance to Christianity that was similar to his earlier resistance to theism. "As strong, but shorter-lived," Lewis tells us, "for I understood it better" (237).

What exactly his "pure and simple" theism consisted of and where its defining characteristics came from, Lewis does not really say. While Jack did not yet believe in the Christ of the New Testament, the God that he now accepted was in many ways like the God of the Bible. He was someone one should kneel, pray, and submit to. Though Jack earnestly desired not to meet him, God earnestly desired to meet Jack. He was someone who, once admitted in, would make demands. These demands would be good and would have to be followed. In these ways, Jack's theism foreshadowed the Christian beliefs he would later embrace.

Lewis tells us in his autobiography that theism made him less self-focused. "I had been, as they say, 'taken out of myself,'" he writes (233). Even if it did nothing else for him, he notes, he would still be thankful that his new belief in God had cured him of the practice of keeping a diary, an activity he now found to be too centered on himself. It is interesting that the only fictional character Lewis creates who will keep a diary will be Eustace Clarence Scrubb in *The Voyage of the Dawn Treader*. Like Jack, Eustace after his conversion abandons his diary—which was for the most part a listing of petty grievances and a catalog of his virtues and the shortcomings of others—and never picks it up again.

Recall the beginning of the passage from the afterword to *The Pilgrim's Regress* mentioned earlier, where Lewis maps out his spiritual journey: "On the intellectual side my own progress had been from 'popular realism' to Philosophical Idealism; from Idealism to . . ." (200). The phrase "on the intellectual side" implies that all along there was another side to his conversion. In *Surprised by Joy*, Lewis also tells us that now his theism did more than take him out of himself: it demanded regular moral evaluation and moral improvement. Any self-examination which occurred now could no longer simply be a pleasant, congratulatory session but became a duty and a spiritual discipline, something that was not comfortable. On January 30, 1930—in between Jack's conversion to theism in 1929 and his acceptance of Christ in 1931—he wrote a long letter to Arthur describing what he now saw when he examined himself. One passage in particular provides an insightful portrait of Jack's spiritual concerns at the time:

> What worries me much more is *Pride*—my besetting sin, as yours is *indolence*. During my afternoon "meditations"—which I at least *attempt* quite regularly now—I have found out ludicrous and terrible things about my own character. Sitting by, watching the rising thoughts . . . one out of every three is a thought of self-admiration. . . . I catch myself posturing before the mirror, so to speak. I pretend I am carefully thinking out what to say to the next pupil (for *his* good, of course) and then suddenly realize I am really thinking how frightfully clever I'm going to be and how he will admire me. I pretend I am remembering an evening of good

fellowship in a really friendly and charitable spirit—and all the time I'm really remembering how good a fellow I am and how well I talked. And then when you force yourself to stop it, you admire yourself for doing *that*. . . . There seems to be no end to it. Depth under depth of self-love and self-admiration. (*CLI*, 878)

Two weeks later, Jack would write Greeves again and return to this topic, comparing himself to an instrument that wants to play itself because "it thinks it knows the tune better than the Musician" (*CLI*, 882).

In *The Voyage of the Dawn Treader*, Eustace is finally able to see how dragonish he has been for most of his life. Finally desiring to change, Eustace—who has literally turned into a dragon—is able to shed the superficial layers of this dragon nature somewhat easily, without much pain, and without any help. The deeper layers will be just the opposite. Eustace finds they are impossible to remove on his own. He cannot undragon himself. He needs Aslan to do it for him.

Jack would have a similar need to allow Christ to help him shed "depth under depth" of self-love and self-admiration—his own act of finally giving the Musician control of the instrument.

One way that Jack's theism differed from his later faith was that it initially included no belief in an afterlife—no hope of eternal reward, no fear of eternal punishment. At this point Lewis reports that he believed that God was to be obeyed simply because he was God.

In *Letters to Malcolm*, Lewis writes to his fictional corre-spondent about this stage when he did not yet embrace the promise of heaven.

You know my history. You know why my withers are quite unwrung by the fear that I was bribed—that I was lured into Christianity by the hope of everlasting life. I believed in God before I believed in Heaven. And even now, even *if*—let's make an impossible supposition—His voice, unmistakably His, said to me, "They have misled you. I can do nothing of the sort for you. . . ." Would that be a moment for changing sides? (120)

In Lewis's point that the promise of eternal life was not the reason he was on God's side, that he would choose God even if there were no heaven, we may be reminded of the scene in *The Silver Chair* where Puddleglum tells the Green Witch, "I'm going to live as like a Narnian as I can even if there isn't any Narnia" (182).

Of course, Jack later came to believe in heaven, but he would see eternal life not as payment for correct behavior but as the consummation of a life of discipleship. In "The Weight of Glory," he explains the difference this way:

> We must not be troubled by unbelievers when they say that this promise of reward makes the Christian life a mercenary affair. There are different kinds of rewards. There is the reward which has no natural connection with the things you do to earn it and is quite foreign to the desires that ought to accompany those things. Money is not the natural reward of love; that is why we call a man mercenary if he marries a woman for the sake of her money. But marriage is the proper reward for a real lover, and he is not mercenary for desiring it. . . . Proper rewards are not simply tacked on to the activity for which they are given, they are the activity itself in consummation. . . . Those who have attained everlasting life in the vision of God doubtless know very well that it is no mere bribe, but the very consummation of their earthly discipleship. (17–18)

Lewis noted that a new Christian might set out initially to do good out of the promise of heaven or fear of hell, like a young student might study in order to receive praise or avoid being punished. But as the student and Christian mature, the former will desire to learn for his or her own sake, and the latter, to do what is right simply because it is right.

But we are getting ahead of ourselves.

On September 25, 1929, Albert died at Little Lea. He had been ill, and Jack had been home the week before. After being reassured that his father was on the mend following surgery for cancer, Jack had returned to Oxford only to receive a telegram with news that Albert had taken a turn for the worse. Jack immediately set out for Belfast again. When he arrived at Little Lea, Albert was already gone. While Lewis assures us in *Surprised by Joy*, "My father's death, with all the fortitude (even playfulness) which he displayed in his last illness, does not really come into the story I am telling" (215), George Sayer suggests that Jack's spiritual journey was influenced by his father's death. Sayer explains:

> He could no longer rebel against the political churchgoing that was part of his father's way of life. He felt bitterly ashamed of the way he had deceived and denigrated his father in the past, and he determined to eradicate these weaknesses in his character. Most importantly, he had a strong feeling that Albert was somehow still alive and helping him. He spoke about this to me and wrote about it to an American correspondent. . . . His feelings of Albert's presence created or reinforced in him a belief in personal immortality and also influenced his conduct in times of temptation. (224)

The American correspondent Sayer refers to is Vera Matthews. In a letter dated March 27, 1951, Lewis wrote to her after she told him news of her father's death. Lewis responded that he hoped she was not trying to pretend, as some high-minded Christians might, that the death did not really matter. About the death of a loved one, Lewis goes on to tell her:

> It matters a great deal, and very solemnly. And for those who are left, the pain is not the whole thing. I feel very strongly (and I am not alone in this) that some great good comes from the dead to

the living in the months or weeks after the death. I think I was much helped by my own father after his death: as if Our Lord welcomed the newly dead with the gift of some power to bless those they have left behind. . . . Certainly, they often seem just at that time, to be very near us. (*CLIII*, 104)

Lewis tells us in *Surprised by Joy* that, as a new convert to theism, he felt morally obligated to make some public statement of the change in his beliefs as a next step: "I thought one ought to 'fly one's flag' by some unmistakable overt sign" (233).

Now how exactly does a new theist—someone who believes only in God, pure and simple—fly his flag? Jack chose to begin attending the local Anglican church, Holy Trinity, on Sundays and the services in the Magdalen chapel on weekdays. Lewis makes a point of telling us that he did this although he neither believed in Christianity nor considered the difference between his theism and Christianity to be small. So why would Jack choose to fly his flag of theism in this way, in what he acknowledges was a merely symbolic action?

Several answers suggest themselves, but since Lewis does not provide further comment, they all must remain speculation. First, while Jack was not a Christian believer yet, it is entirely likely he already had leanings this way—leanings caused by his upbringing, his friends, and his favorite authors. Lewis tells us in *Surprised by Joy* that to accept the incarnation was a step further in the same direction his theism had taken him. Second, in joining the worshipers at Holy Trinity and at college chapel, he would have joined people who shared his belief in God. They were Christian theists, and he was a "pure and simple" theist, but they were all in the theist camp. Lewis honored the point where they parted ways by not taking Communion with them. Finally, there would certainly have been plenty of atheists at Oxford. By attending services at Holy Trinity and the college chapel, Jack wanted to make it clear that he was no longer one of them.

There may have been some who attended these services because they liked the ritual, the beauty of the music, or the liturgy. Jack was not one of them. Lewis explains in his autobiography that he was not just antiecclesiastical but *deeply* antiecclesiastical, and in this delightful passage he provides his long list of objections to attending church:

> It was . . . a wearisome "get-together" affair. I couldn't yet see how a concern of that sort should have anything to do with one's spiritual life. To me, religion ought to have been a matter of good men praying alone and meeting by twos and threes to talk of spiritual matters. And then the fussy, time-wasting botheration of it all! The bells, the crowds, the umbrellas, the notices, the bustle, the perpetual arranging and organizing. Hymns were (and are) extremely disagreeable to me. Of all musical instruments I liked (and like) the organ least. I have, too, a sort of spiritual *gaucherie* which makes me unapt to participate in any rite. (234)

And yet despite all his objections, despite the fact that he was not a Christian yet, Jack felt the need to fly his flag by attending. And so the most dejected and reluctant convert in all of England became England's most dejected and reluctant churchgoer.

T. D. Weldon's comment, which back in 1926 had shaken Jack's view of what was possible, now turned him toward considering the historical accuracy of the Gospel accounts of Jesus. Had all that about the dying god really happened once on a hill outside of Jerusalem? In *Mere Christianity* Lewis writes, "I am not asking anyone to accept Christianity if his best reasoning tells him that the weight of the evidence is against it" (140). Now Jack carefully and without prejudice reconsidered the evidence of the New Testament record. In his autobiography, Lewis reports on the conclusion he was gradually drawn to.

> If ever a myth had become fact, had been incarnated, it would be just like this. And nothing else in all literature was just like this.

Myths were like it in one way. Histories were like it in another. But nothing was simply like it. And no person was like the Person it depicted; as real, as recognizable . . . as Plato's Socrates or Boswell's Johnson . . . , yet also numinous, lit by a light from beyond the world, . . . not a god, but God. Here and here only in all time the myth must have become fact. (236)

In his address "Christian Apologetics," Lewis advised a conference of Anglican priests and youth leaders on how they might help bring others to the faith, and spoke of the role the evidence from the New Testament had played in his own conversion. "One of the great difficulties is to keep before the audience's mind the question of truth," he told the audience. "They always think you are recommending Christianity not because it is *true* but because it is *good*" (101). Lewis then concluded with this assertion: "Christianity is a statement which, if false, is of *no* importance, and, if true, of infinite importance. The one thing it cannot be is moderately important."

Lewis's most famous statement about the historical Jesus—often called the liar, lunatic, or Lord trilemma—is found in *Mere Christianity*. Lewis writes:

I am trying here to prevent anyone saying the really foolish thing that people often say about Him: "I'm ready to accept Jesus as a great moral teacher, but I don't accept his claim to be God." That is the one thing we must not say. A man who was merely a man and said the sort of things Jesus said would not be a great moral teacher. He would either be a lunatic—on the level with the man who says he is a poached egg—or else he would be the Devil of Hell. You must make your choice. Either this man was, and is, the Son of God, or else a madman or something worse. You can shut Him up for a fool, you can spit at Him and kill Him as a demon; or you can fall at His feet and call Him Lord and God. But let us not come with any patronizing nonsense about His being a great human teacher. He has not left that open to us. (52)

If his conversation five years earlier with Weldon about the historical evidence from the Gospels now became one factor in Jack's final step of faith, a second conversation would play an even more important role—a conversation quite well known among Lewis fans. On September 19, 1931, Jack, Hugo Dyson, and Tolkien talked late into the night as they strolled Addison's Walk, the wooded path that runs alongside the Magdalen grounds. Though Lewis does not mention it in *Surprised by Joy*, the myth-become-fact passage quoted earlier came directly out of this conversation. Our record of what happened that night comes from three letters Jack wrote to Arthur Greeves.

In the first letter, dated September 22, 1931, Lewis explains that he could not write earlier because he had a weekend guest staying with him, Hugo Dyson, who at the time was teaching English at the University of Reading. Tolkien had joined them for dinner, and afterward the three of them went for a walk. Tolkien stayed until three in the morning. Dyson and Jack continued talking until four as they walked up and down the cloister of New Building.

In this first letter, Jack provides Greeves with only the mere basics about their talk. "We began (in Addison's walk just after dinner) on metaphor and myth," Lewis writes (*CLI*, 970). He then describes how they were interrupted by a mystical rush of wind that was so unexpected and so out of place on the still, warm evening that they were all startled and held their breaths. "We continued (in my room) on Christianity: a good long satisfying talk in which I learned a lot," Lewis further reports. But he stops there and says no more about this long talk or about what it was he learned.

Nine days later, on October 1, Jack wrote Arthur again. This time he includes a few more details, but, given the announcement he makes, again they seem surprisingly scant: "I have just passed on from believing in God to definitely believing in Christ—in

Christianity. I will try to explain this another time. My long talk with Dyson and Tolkien had a good deal to do with it" (*CLI*, 974).

On October 18, Jack wrote to Arthur once more and finally gives him a full description of what happened on that late night walk and how the obstacle which had been keeping him from belief had been overcome.

> Now what Dyson and Tolkien showed me was this: that if I met the idea of sacrifice in a Pagan story I didn't mind it at all: again, that if I met the idea of a god sacrificing himself to himself . . . I liked it very much and was mysteriously moved by it: again, that the idea of the dying and reviving god . . . similarly moved me provided I met it anywhere *except* in the Gospels. . . . Now the story of Christ is simply a true myth: a myth working on us in the same way as the others, but with this tremendous difference that *it really happened*. (*CLI*, 976–77)

Tolkien and Dyson helped Jack see the historical as well as the spiritual truth of the Gospel story. They also helped him to see a new and deeper value in the myths from other traditions. Jack wrote to Arthur that he now saw Pagan myths as "God expressing Himself through the minds of poets, using such images as He found there" (*CLI*, 977). Jack did not have to reject what he had loved so much in "Tegner's Drapa," *Siegfried*, or *The Tale of Squirrel Nutkin*. If anything, he could even love and embrace these works more as glimpses of divine truth. Later, in *Miracles*, Lewis would describe what Tolkien and Dyson had helped him to understand in this way:

> Myth in general is not merely misunderstood history (as Euhemerus thought) nor diabolical illusion (as some of the Fathers thought) or priestly lying (as the philosophers of the Enlightenment thought) but, at its best, a real though unfocused gleam of divine truth falling on human imagination. (134)

The idea of the dying and reviving god . . . moved me provided I met it anywhere except in the Gospels. In the final words of this statement, we can hear Jack's bias against Christianity. Tolkien heard it as well and would not let it go uncorrected. This is the same bias found earlier in Jack's statements about Chesterton and Herbert. It took a close friend to point out this deeply ingrained anti-Christian prejudice, a friend Jack thoroughly trusted and whose opinion he had the utmost respect for.

And so we have one of the world's greatest stories of literary friendship. Without Tolkien's Christian influence, there might have been no *Screwtape Letters* or Narnia. Similarly, without Lewis's encouragement, there might have been no *Lord of the Rings*, for when Tolkien got discouraged and stopped altogether, Jack was there insisting on more.

On the morning of September 28, 1931—nine days after his late-night talk with Tolkien and Dyson—Jack took the final step to belief. Lewis warns us in *Surprised by Joy* that while he can say exactly when this final step was taken, he can hardly say how. And so what he can tell us is striking in its brevity. Lewis simply reports: "I was driven to Whipsnade one sunny morning. When we set out I did not believe that Jesus Christ is the Son of God, and when we reached the zoo I did" (237). Lewis comments that he had not spent the trip in deep thought or in great emotion. Like the decision on the bus top, there was a peculiar calmness and peace that accompanied this momentous resolution.

And so Jack became a believer, not while sitting in a wooden pew at Holy Trinity or during matins in Magdalen's Renaissance chapel, not while kneeling beside his bed or on one of his beloved walks in the rural countryside, not while reading Northern mythology or in the middle of a book by a favorite Christian writer, but while whizzing past farms and fields in the sidecar of Warnie's motorcycle. And while this was the end of a long, sometimes winding spiritual journey, it was also, as Lewis suggests in the chapter title, the beginning of another.

What were these last few steps to Christianity like? As he usually does, Lewis communicates his deepest truths through metaphors we can imagine or pictures we can see. On the bus going up Headington Hill, Jack was like a lobster, or a man wearing armor, who was given the chance to remove his defensive shell. Having made the decision to unbuckle, he was then like a snowman beginning to melt and like a fox chased out of the woods. The long process was like an angler playing a fish that did not even know it had been hooked. It was like a game of chess where, one by one, Jack's pieces were put in disarray and captured, a game which ended in checkmate.

Now, in the final step, as he came to believe that Jesus Christ is the Son of God, Lewis writes that it was like when "a man, after long sleep, still lying motionless in bed, becomes aware that he is now awake" (237).

In his memoir, Warnie rejects one picture of Jack's conversion that day and offers one of his own, writing: "I well remember that day in 1931 when we made a visit to Whipsnade Zoo, Jack riding in my sidecar. . . . This seemed to me no sudden plunge into a new life, but rather a slow steady convalescence from a deep-seated spiritual illness of long standing" (39).

Lewis finishes the very last page of *Surprised by Joy* with two final images. Upon reaching the zoo, he and Warnie found songbirds singing overhead, bluebells blooming underfoot, and wallabies hopping on their powerful hind legs all around them. Lewis writes that this setting, combined with his newfound belief in Christ, was almost like Eden come again.

And so we have come full circle from the opening epigraph in chapter 1—Milton's line describing Adam and Eve's precarious bliss in paradise: "Happy, but for so happy ill secured." On the road to Whipsnade, Jack found a new kind of happiness to replace the one he lost as a boy—this one well secured.

This one, paradise regained.

"But what, in conclusion, of Joy?" Lewis asks. "For that, after all is what the story has mainly been about" (238). Lewis announces that the topic has lost nearly all interest for him since he became a Christian. This is not because he has ceased experiencing Joy like he used to—quite the contrary. Lewis tells us that the old stab has come as often and as sharply as any time before. But now he recognizes Joy "only as a pointer to something other and outer." In his final image, he compares his situation to a group that is on a journey. When they are lost in the woods, a condition which suggests Jack's preconversion stage, the sight of a signpost is itself a great matter. But once they are back on the road to their destination, with signposts every few miles, no one wants to stop or take much notice of them—no matter how glorious these signposts are. Lewis concludes this final metaphor with words borrowed from *The Scale of Perfection* by the fourteenth-century English mystic Walter Hilton: "We would be at Jerusalem."

And so the years from 1925 to 1931, which Jack began as an idealist not quite free of his New Look, ended with him a new convert to Christianity. In the preface for *God in the Dock*, Walter Hooper would later observe: "Lewis struck me as the most thoroughly *converted* man I ever met. Christianity was never for him a separate department of life, nor what he did with his solitude. . . . His whole vision of life was such that the natural and the supernatural seemed inseparably combined" (12).

In the final interview Lewis gave—one which took place in his rooms at Cambridge on May 7, 1963, and was later published under the title "Cross Examination"—he looked back on this final stage of his conversion and commented: "I feel my decision was not so important. I was the object rather than the subject in this affair. I was decided upon. I was glad afterwards at the way it came out, but at the moment what I heard was God saying: 'Put down your gun and we'll talk'" (261).

There would be more steps for Jack to take on his spiritual journey in the years after 1931, but rather than separate steps or distinct stages, these would be steps which continued on in the right direction—steps further on the road to Jerusalem.

Steps further up and further in.

5

Inkling and Author

(1 9 3 1 – 1 9 5 0)

On Thursday we had a meeting of the Inklings. . . . I have never in my life seen Dyson so exuberant—"a roaring cataract of nonsense." The bill of fare afterwards consisted of a section of the new Hobbit book from Tolkien, a nativity play from Williams (unusually intelligible for him, and approved by all), and a chapter out of the book on the Problem of Pain from me.

—*Collected Letters*, volume 2

The New Convert

At the end of *The Voyage of the Dawn Treader*, Aslan cheers a disheartened Lucy, who has just been told she is too old to come back to Narnia, by telling her that he can be found in her world as well. "But there I have another name," the great lion explains. "You must learn to know me by that name" (247). It could be said that Jack, following his decision on the road to Whipsnade that crisp fall day in September 1931, would spend his remaining thirty-two years learning to know Aslan by the name he is known by in our world.

Early on Christmas morning 1931, Jack walked from the Kilns to Holy Trinity Church to attend the eight o'clock service. The winding half mile down the tree-lined streets in the faint predawn light was not a long distance, but it would mark the endpoint of one long journey and the starting point of another. Jack had been attending matins and evensong services at Holy Trinity since becoming a theist two years before, but on this special morning he took the next step in flying his flag of faith by attending the celebration of the Eucharist with the rest of the believers.

There is a passage in the Church of England's Book of Common Prayer which contains the words "Christ our Passover is sacrificed for us: therefore let us keep the feast." Jack had a favorite pew he sat in at Holy Trinity—one chosen because it was next to a column that could partially hide him. When Warnie retired and came home from the service, he would join his brother there. On this Christmas morning, Jack got up from the pew and went to the front of the church with his fellow Christians, where they knelt together to keep the feast.

And unlike when he took the Sacrament at his confirmation and first Communion seventeen years before at St. Mark's, this time Jack really believed in Christ and his sacrifice.

In a strange coincidence, halfway around the world, Warnie, who was stationed in Shanghai at the time, also received Communion on this day for the first time in a long time.

Since different denominations schedule Communion services at different intervals—some daily and others far less often—in his published writing, Lewis was careful *not* to state his preference for how often he thought one should partake. And, in fact, his own practice changed over the years. Warnie reports in his memoir that at one point, after his brother had been a practicing Christian for some time, Jack told him that taking the Sacrament once a month seemed to strike the right balance between "enthusiasm and Laodiceanism" (40), but in later years he changed his opinion and took Communion every week and on major feast days.

With Lewis's story of his conversion in *Surprised by Joy* at an end, we now must turn to other sources to trace his spiritual biography. His letters now play a larger role in this task. Lewis wrote hundreds, and refers to spiritual topics more frequently. He also traces his journey in two other autobiographical works. The first, *The Pilgrim's Regress*, was published just two years after his conversion. The second, *A Grief Observed*, came out three decades after the life-changing ride to the zoo in Warnie's sidecar.

We can also find markers of Lewis's further spiritual journey in the astonishing number of Christian works—both fiction and apologetic—which poured from his pen in the years from 1932 to 1963. For example, in *Letters to Malcolm* we learn a good deal about his prayer life. At one point Lewis suggests that while most Christians find prayer to be a simple matter, he himself did not—not at the start. "What is more natural, and easier, if you believe in God, than to address Him?" he first asks (77). Well, it may depend on who you are and where you are coming from, Lewis goes on to suggest: "For those in my position—adult converts from the *intelligentsia*—that simplicity and spontaneity can't always be the starting point. One can't just jump back into one's childhood. . . . We have to work back to the simplicity a long way round."

As we have seen, Lewis chooses not to say anything in *Surprised by Joy* about his relationship with Mrs. Moore. In addition, he says almost nothing about his father's death except to report it. Lewis also does not say anything in his autobiography about the two books of poetry he published in his twenties—works that, to borrow words from Alexander Pope, were damned with faint praise by critics. While there were several young British soldiers who became famous war poets—figures such as Wilfred Owen and Siegfried Sassoon—Lewis was not one of them. Shakespeare's declaration that "sweet are the uses of adversity" is relevant again. Had *Spirits in Bondage* (1919) or *Dymer* (1926) received more praise, Jack might have spent the next decade writing philosophical poetry. Instead, he turned to a very different kind of writing soon after his conversion.

On August 18, 1930—a year after he had knelt and admitted God was God but a year before accepting Christ—Jack wrote to Arthur Greeves concerning how he felt about his previous goal of becoming, not just a poet, but a famous poet.

> From the age of sixteen onwards I had one single ambition, from which I never wavered, in the prosecution of which I spent every ounce I could, on which I really and deliberately staked my whole contentment: and I recognize myself as having unmistakably failed in it. . . . The side of me which longs, not to write, for no one can stop us doing that, but to be approved as a writer, is not the side of us that is really worth much. (*CLI*, 925–26)

And so Jack continued to write after his conversion, but now did so mostly for writing's sake. He gave up—or worked on giving up—that side of him that wrote in order to win acclaim. Then, in August 1932, Jack went to Ireland for a holiday, and during this time he stayed with Greeves, since Little Lea had been sold after Albert's death. In an amazing two-week span, he completed the entire manuscript of *The Pilgrim's Regress*, the allegorical tale of a pilgrim who traces Jack's own steps to belief. Richard Wagner offers this summary of the convoluted tale:

The Pilgrim's Regress focuses on a man, named John, who lives an empty life in a land called Puritania. After seeing a vision of a beautiful island, an intense longing fills him and makes John immediately want to try and find it. . . . His odyssey leads him to many different detours and destinations, but he encounters false joy in one place after another. Physical sins, spiritual sins, and various philosophical movements all become dead ends and never fulfill him. (230)

Near the end of *The Pilgrim's Regress*, we come to a chapter titled "Securus Te Projice," which is Latin for "throw yourself away without care" and an allusion to the words that Augustine heard before his own plunge into faith. There John tells Mother Kirk—a character who stands for Christianity, Lewis explains—that he has come to give himself up. In words that echo Lewis's later account of his own conversion, Mother Kirk tells the reluctant convert, "You have come a long way round to reach this place" (166). She then tells him that all that remains for him to do is to take off his grimy rags and dive into the pool of water that lies before him.

The Pilgrim's Regress and his two earlier books of poetry are Lewis's least successful works. It is safe to say hardly anyone today would know them had he not gone on to write better books. Millions of copies of Lewis's works are in print today. By contrast, the first printing of *The Pilgrim's Regress* was a mere 1,000 copies. Of these, only around 650 were initially sold. Part of the problem was that the public's taste for allegory had greatly diminished in the years since 1678, when John Bunyan wrote *The Pilgrim's Progress*. Lewis's needless obscurity, mentioned earlier, was another factor in its lack of sales. Nevertheless, with its shift from poetry to prose and its evidence of Lewis's newly converted worldview, *Regress* was a start—a hint, but only that, of what was to come.

The Pilgrim's Regress was published in May 1933 with the dedication to Arthur Greeves it still bears today. Jack would

go on to have more famous friends—*The Problem of Pain*
(1940) would be dedicated to the Inklings; *The Screwtape Letters* (1942), to J. R. R. Tolkien; and *A Preface to Paradise Lost*
(1942), to Charles Williams—but he would have no better friend
than Arthur over the next three decades of his life, nor anyone
except his brother that he would be friends with longer.

As mentioned earlier, in the preface to the 1960 edition of
Screwtape, Lewis makes it clear that any insights he can provide
about how temptation works came not from long years studying
theological texts but from his own heart. Given this statement, if
we now turn to Screwtape's letters, we can find several obstacles
encountered by Wormwood's new convert which trace Jack's
early steps after his own conversion.

"The Enemy will be working from the center outwards,"
Screwtape observes, "gradually bringing more and more of the
patient's conduct under the new standard" (11). Certainly this
was Jack's experience as, gradually, the layers of self-love and
self-admiration he had written about to Arthur were exposed
and peeled away.

One of the first areas Wormwood is advised to exploit is his
patient's relations with his mother—in particular the friction
caused by the new convert's churchgoing and the radical change
in his values and interests. "Is she at all jealous of the new factor
in her son's life? . . . Does she feel he is making a great deal of
'fuss' about it?" Screwtape asks (14).

In fact, Mrs. Moore was at times quite jealous of her adopted son's new faith. Biographers Green and Hooper include
Owen Barfield's account of her mocking Jack and Warnie about
the "blood feasts" they participated in at Holy Trinity on Sundays (233). In a diary entry for December 21, 1933, two years
after Jack's conversion, Warnie records that Mrs. Moore was
nagging his brother about having become a believer.

In an interview he gave in 1944, later published as "Answers to Questions on Christianity," Lewis was asked if attendance at a place of worship or membership with a Christian community was necessary to a Christian way of life. In his response, he alludes to Mrs. Moore's resentment of his churchgoing.

> My own experience is that when I first became a Christian, about fourteen years ago, I thought that I could do it on my own, by retiring to my rooms and reading theology, and I wouldn't go to the churches and Gospel Halls; and then later I found that it was the only way of flying your flag. . . . It is extraordinary how inconvenient to your family it becomes for you to get up early to go to church. It doesn't matter so much if you get up early for anything else, but if you get up early to go to church it's very selfish of you and you upset the house. (61)

Nevertheless, Jack persisted—despite Mrs. Moore's objections and his own disinclinations.

The Oxford area offered the newly converted Jack the usual array of church choices. Would he join a Catholic church, or would he opt for a Protestant one? If Protestant, which denomination? And, after deciding on the denomination, would he attend a church with more elaborate and formal services, or one less ritualized and simpler?

In the preface to *Mere Christianity*, Lewis describes himself as "a very ordinary layman of the church of England" and as not especially high or low—or "especially anything else" (viii). But we never learn exactly how Jack chose the Anglican Church or what factors made him neither especially high church nor especially low church. This lack of personal information was intentional on his part. Lewis concludes the preface by saying that it is not his goal to tell anyone what church to join: "You will not learn from me whether you ought to become an Anglican, a Methodist, a Presbyterian, or a Roman Catholic."

That said, Lewis favored joining *some* denomination—going through one door, as he puts it—and offers this advice:

> You must be asking which door is the true one; not which pleases you best by its paint and paneling. In plain language, the question should never be: "Do I like that kind of service?" but "Are these doctrines true: Is holiness here? Does my conscience move me towards this? Is my reluctance to knock at this door due to my pride, or my mere taste, or my personal dislike of this particular door-keeper?" (xvi)

Assuming that its doctrines were true and holiness was present, Lewis favored the parochial principle, where a new convert simply attends his or her local parish church. In letter 16, Screwtape advocates the opposite view, telling Wormwood that if his patient cannot be cured of churchgoing, the next best thing is to send him looking for a church that "suits" him and so make him into a "taster or connoisseur" of churches (81).

In this search for a suitable church, Screwtape notes, the new convert can be made to become a critic when God intends for him to be a pupil. Instead of church being a place that brings together people of different classes and different tastes, Screwtape tells Wormwood that he is to turn it into a coterie or club.

And so while Jack could have chosen to attend services at the beautiful cathedral at Oxford's Christ Church College—where the preaching might have been more learned, the music more accomplished, and the other churchgoers more sophisticated—he chose to attend Holy Trinity, the modest church in his parish. It is likely that at least some of the following description Lewis has Screwtape give about Wormwood's patient was autobiographical:

> When he goes inside, he sees the local grocer with rather an oily expression on his face bustling up to offer him one shiny little book containing a liturgy . . . and one shabby little book containing corrupt texts of a number of religious lyrics, mostly

bad, and in very small print. When he gets to his pew and looks round him he sees just that selection of his neighbors whom he has hitherto avoided. (6–7)

These elements are all part of the anticlimax which Screwtape is certain will come in the patient's first few weeks after joining the church. Several pages later, Screwtape devotes an entire letter to this topic of spiritual disappointments, or troughs, as he calls them.

As a new convert, Jack experienced these struggles as well. In "Answers to Questions on Christianity," Lewis describes his early experiences attending church: "I disliked very much their hymns, which I considered to be fifth-rate poems set to sixth-rate music. But as I went on I saw the great merit of it. I came up against different people of quite different outlooks and different education, and then gradually my conceit just began peeling off" (61–62). Initially put off by an old man next to him in elastic-side work boots, Lewis concludes, "Then you realize that you aren't fit to clean those boots."

In letter 21, Screwtape writes that although Wormwood's patient is, as a new convert, committed in theory to a "total service of the Enemy," the junior devil is to try to keep alive in him the curious assumption that "my time is my own" (112). "You will have noticed," Screwtape points out, "that nothing throws him into a passion so easily as to find a tract of time which he reckoned on having at his own disposal unexpectedly taken from him" (111).

In *The Problem of Pain*, Lewis further describes the "my time is my own" problem and includes himself as someone who struggled with it after his conversion gave him, as he calls it in this passage, a new center.

> From the moment a creature becomes aware of God as God and
> of itself as self, the terrible alternative of choosing God or self

for the center is opened to it. . . . We try, when we wake, to lay
the new day at God's feet; before we have finished shaving, it
becomes *our* day and God's share in it is felt as a tribute which
we must pay out of "our own" pocket, a deduction from the
time which ought, we feel, to be "our own." (66–67)

If Lewis the new convert includes *obstacles* for Wormwood's
patient which he also faced himself, he also includes the *joys
and triumphs* of a new convert. In letter 13, the patient experiences a return to grace after enjoying two of Jack's greatest
pleasures: reading a favorite book and taking a walk. One of
the things Jack discovered after his conversion was that while
God wanted in one sense to change him entirely, in another
sense God had created him in a unique way and valued that
uniqueness. Screwtape explains the seeming paradox this way:

> Of course I know that the Enemy also wants to detach men
> from themselves, but in a different way. Remember always, that
> He really likes the little vermin, and sets an absurd value on
> the distinctness of every one of them. When He talks of their
> losing their selves, He only means abandoning the clamor of
> self-will; once they have done that, He really gives them back all
> their personality, and boasts (I am afraid, sincerely) that when
> they are wholly His they will be more themselves than ever. (65)

Jack found that as he abandoned his self-will, as his new
faith required, God allowed him to keep his distinct, personal
tastes and that he was, we could say, more himself than ever.

In the *Mere Christianity* section titled "The New Men," Lewis
asks readers to consider a comparison which he admits is not the
best analogy: As new Christians gradually become new people,
yes, they must in one sense lose themselves. But in another sense,
Lewis proposes, it is like putting salt on an egg or cabbage. Salt
actually helps bring out their special taste. Echoing the point
made in *Screwtape*, Lewis concludes, "The more we get what

we now call 'ourselves' out of the way and let Him take us over, the more truly ourselves we become" (225).

And so Jack the new convert gradually became Jack the new man, the man he was always meant to be—the Oxford don who, more than ever, loved his walks in the country, his cup of tea and pint of beer, his ancient myths, and, most of all, his times of talking and laughing with friends.

The Oxford Inklings

On December 3, 1929, Jack wrote to Arthur that he had gotten himself into "a whirl," as he always did at the end of the term (*CLI*, 838). At this point he had just turned thirty-one and had been a fellow at Magdalen for four years. He then provides Arthur with this dizzying description of the many activities, besides his lectures and tutorials, he was involved in:

> I have too many irons in the fire—the Michaelmas Club, the Linguistic Society, and the Icelandic Society. . . . One week I was up till 2:30 on Monday (talking to the Anglo Saxon professor Tolkien who came with me to College from a society and sat discoursing of the gods and giants and Asgard for three hours, then departing in the wind and rain—who could turn him out, for the fire was bright and the talk good?), next night till 1:00 talking to someone else, and on Wednesday till 12:00 with the Icelandics. It is very hard to keep one's feet in this sea of engagements.

Notably missing from Jack's list of engagements is any mention of a meeting of the Inklings, the legendary reading-and-writing group he came to be associated with. The reason it is missing is that the Inklings would not be formed until the next year, and even then it would take until 1933 for it to become the group that we think of today.

When Tolkien was in his midseventies and beginning to witness his works acquire worldwide fame, he received a question about how the Inklings meetings began and where the name came from. In a letter dated September 11, 1967, he offers the following response:

> The name was not invented by C. S. L. (nor by me). In origin it was an undergraduate jest, devised as the name of a literary (or writer's) club. The founder was an undergraduate at University College, named Tangye-Lean. . . . Both C. S. L. and I became members. The club met in T.-L.'s room in University College: its procedure was that at each meeting members should read aloud, unpublished compositions. These were supposed to be open to immediate criticism. . . . The club soon died. . . . Its name was then transferred (by C. S. L.) to the undetermined and unelected circle of friends who gathered about C. S. L., and met in his rooms in Magdalen. (387–88)

Tolkien goes on to state that because of Lewis's great passion for hearing things read aloud, this second manifestation of the Inklings would have come into existence with or without the existence of the original short-lived club whose name it assumed after Tangye-Lean graduated.

In *The Four Loves* section titled "Friendship," Lewis provides a general explanation of how the Inklings and similar groups of friends came into being. Lewis maintains that friendship arises from mere companionship when two or more of the companions discover they share in common "some insight or interest or even taste which the others do not" (65). He invites us to imagine a group of companions with a common study, a common profession, or a common recreation. Here we might picture the faculty members that Lewis and Tolkien taught with at Oxford. While all who share this common aspect will be our companions, Lewis notes, "one or two or three who share something more will be our Friends" (66). Lewis gives *friends* a capital letter to make it clear he means something special by the term. "The Friends will still be doing something together but something more inward, less widely shared and less easily defined."

Lewis then paints a moving portrait of a circle of friends, and it is hard not to assume that he had the Inklings in mind.

> Each member of the circle feels, in his secret heart, humbled before all the rest. Sometimes he wonders what he is doing there among his betters. He is lucky beyond desert to be in such company. Especially when the whole group is together, each bringing out all that is best, wisest, or funniest in all the others . . . ; when the whole world, and something beyond the world, opens itself to our minds as we talk. (66)

In her book *The Company They Keep: C. S. Lewis and J. R. R. Tolkien as Writers in Community*, Diana Pavlac Glyer proposes that the Inklings actually had their real origins not when Lean's club disbanded in 1933, but four years earlier.

> To the extent that there is one critical moment in the formation of the Inklings as a group, it seems to be the moment in December 1929 when Tolkien made the courageous decision to share his created mythology with Lewis. From there, a casual pattern was established as Tolkien and Lewis began meeting to read and critique each other's works. These meetings received a boost in 1931, when Lewis renewed his Christian faith, and another when Warren Lewis retired in 1932 and moved to Oxford. (11)

Following their late-night discussion of gods, giants, and Asgard mentioned in Lewis's December 3 letter to Arthur, Tolkien had given Jack a portion of an unfinished epic poem for comment. It was something he had been working on for a number of years and told of the love of an interracial couple—Beren, a man and a mighty warrior, and Luthien, a fair elf-maiden—and of their adventures in a world called Middle-earth. Jack read it on the evening of December 6, 1929, and the following day he wrote Tolkien that it had been ages since he had an evening of such delight. Jack praised its mythical value and also found a deep sense of reality in the poem's background.

While millions of readers everywhere would come to value and love Tolkien's stories of Middle-earth, Jack was the first. Had Jack not recognized and encouraged the genius which was apparent even in these early drafts, the rest of the world might never have had the chance to see it.

In the years to come, while Jack's works would pour from his pen quickly and seemingly effortlessly, *The Lord of the Rings* would be laboriously written, read aloud to the Inklings, and then laboriously rewritten over the twelve years between 1937 and 1949. Tolkien never finished "The Lay of Leithian," the longer work which the poem he gave Jack was a part of. But in *The Fellowship of the Ring*, finally published in 1954, when Sam asks for a tale about the elves, Tolkien has Aragorn recite lines describing the meeting of Beren son of Barahir and Luthien Tinuviel.

The group that gathered in Lewis's rooms on Thursday nights to read their works aloud, and that met in one of Oxford's pubs for conversation on Tuesday mornings before lunch—most often at the Eagle and Child—never had an official list of members. By Glyer's count, nineteen men, many of whom came and went, could claim to be an Inkling. Among them were Jack, Warnie, Tolkien, Tolkien's son Christopher, Owen Barfield, Nevill Coghill, Hugo Dyson, and Charles Williams. Glyer points out that, despite the large roster, "a typical Thursday night Inklings meeting was fairly small. On the average, six or seven men would show up" (11).

It is not possible to give a full account here of the interactions, contributions, evolution, and influence of the group the world remembers as the Oxford Inklings, who met for fifteen years, from 1934 to 1949. Readers interested in learning more about this amazing collection of thinkers, writers, and friends might look to *The Inklings*, Humphrey Carpenter's book-length treatment of the subject, or to Diana Glyer's definitive work.

Three further comments will conclude our look at the group which produced some of the best writing of its century—some would say of any century.

The first comment comes from Warnie. Toward the middle of his memoir, seeking to dispel the myth that his brother lived the life of a "solitary and embittered recluse" (33), Warnie offers a description of Jack's extraordinary capacity for friendship and of the extraordinary circle which gathered around him. "As all his friends will bear witness," Warnie points out, "he was a man with an outstanding gift for pastime with good company, for laughter and the love of friends."

Warnie then provides what may be the best surviving description of a typical meeting of the Inklings.

> There were no rules, officers, agendas, or formal elections— unless one counts it as a rule that we met in Jack's rooms at Magdalen every Thursday evening after dinner. Proceedings neither began nor terminated at any fixed hour, though there was a tacit agreement that ten-thirty was as late as one could decently arrive. From time to time we added to our original number, but without formalities. . . .
>
> The ritual of an Inklings was unvarying. When half a dozen or so had arrived, tea would be produced, and then when pipes were well alight Jack would say, "Well, has nobody got anything to read us?" Out would come a manuscript, and we would settle down to sit in judgment upon it—real unbiased judgment, too, since we were no mutual admiration society: praise for good work was unstinted, but censure for bad work—or even not-so-good work—was often brutally frank. To read to the Inklings was a formidable ordeal. (33–34)

Warnie concludes by recalling his fear when he read aloud the first chapter of his own book—about France during the reign of Louis XIV—and the delight he felt with the warm reception it received.

The second comment comes from Lewis himself. When World War II broke out, Warnie was called back into service and stationed in Yorkshire. Through regular correspondence, sometimes quite lengthy, Jack endeavored to keep his brother informed about local events. In a letter to Warnie dated November 11, 1939, Jack writes:

> On Thursday we had a meeting of the Inklings. . . . I have never in my life seen Dyson so exuberant—"a roaring cataract of nonsense." The bill of fare afterwards consisted of a section of the new Hobbit book from Tolkien, a nativity play from Williams (unusually intelligible for him, and approved by all), and a chapter out of the book on the Problem of Pain from me. (*CLII*, 288–89)

The "new Hobbit book" Lewis mentions was an early draft of what would become *The Lord of the Rings*. Originally intended merely as a sequel to the adventures of Bilbo Baggins as told in *The Hobbit* published two years earlier, the new story grew in the telling into something quite different in tone, scope, and intent. The unusually intelligible nativity play by Charles Williams was *The House by the Stable*. Lewis reports that the three readings that night almost seemed to fit together in a logical sequence. Borrowing a phrase from Pope's *Essay on Man*, he wishes Warnie could have been there to enjoy a "first-rate evening's talk of the usual wide-ranging kind—'from grave to gay, from lively to severe'" (*CLII*, 289).

The third and final comment comes from Tolkien and focuses not on the general influence and encouragement of the Inklings but on that of Jack in particular.

Though born in 1892, six years before Lewis, Tolkien would outlive him by a decade. Several days after Jack's funeral, Tolkien wrote to his daughter, Priscilla, that while in recent years he had been feeling like an old tree losing its leaves one by one, this loss was like "an ax-blow near the roots" (341). In correspondence two years later, Tolkien describes the "unpayable debt" he owed Lewis, explaining: "He was for long my only audience. Only from him did I ever get the idea that my 'stuff' could be more than a private hobby. But for his interest and unceasing eagerness for more I should never have brought *The Lord of the Rings* to a conclusion" (362).

The Eagle and Child has added more rooms in the back since the days when the Inklings met there, but Lewis fans can still have an order of fish and chips and something to drink in the Rabbit Room where Jack and his circle of friends used to assemble. Though smoking is now prohibited, it is said that if you go there on a Tuesday morning about an hour before lunch, you may detect a whiff of smoke from a distant pipe or perhaps hear a far-off echo of laughter—faint but exuberant.

Famous Christian Author: The 1940s

In the preface he was asked to write for *The Taste of the Pineapple*, a book of essays on Lewis, Owen Barfield comments on the extraordinary breadth of abilities that his friend displayed as a writer. Barfield writes that someone

> who had never had any personal contact with Lewis, but who, omitting the biographical parts, had read the whole or most of what has been written about him, might be pardoned for wondering if it were not one writer, but three with whom he was becoming acquainted: three men who just happened to have the same name and same peculiar vigor of thought and utterance. Such a reader . . . might, to avoid confusion, adopt the nomenclature L1, L2, and L3. L1 being a distinguished and original literary critic, L2 a highly successful author of

fiction, and L3 the writer and broadcaster of popular Christian apologetics. (1)

Below is the amazing list of books that Lewis authored in the first half of his career, through the 1940s. Each is shown along with its genre and the year it was published.

Spirits in Bondage (poetry, 1919)

Dymer (poetry, 1926)

The Pilgrim's Regress (allegory, 1933)

The Allegory of Love (literary criticism, 1936)

Out of the Silent Planet (science fiction, 1938)

The Personal Heresy (literary criticism, 1939)

The Problem of Pain (apologetics, 1940)

The Screwtape Letters (fiction, 1942)

A Preface to Paradise Lost (literary criticism, 1942)

Broadcast Talks (apologetics—part of what would later be *Mere Christianity*, 1942)

Christian Behavior (apologetics—part of what would later be *Mere Christianity*, 1943)

Perelandra (science fiction, 1943)

The Abolition of Man (apologetics, 1943)

Beyond Personality (apologetics—part of what would later be *Mere Christianity*, 1944)

That Hideous Strength (science fiction, 1945)

The Great Divorce (fiction, 1946)

Miracles (apologetics, 1947)

It is beyond the scope and the purpose of this book to provide an in-depth look at the origins and content of each of the—depending on how one counts them—thirty-odd books Lewis wrote during his lifetime. Readers who want to learn more will find that Walter Hooper has done a superb job of providing these things in *C. S. Lewis: A Companion and Guide*. Instead, we will focus on selected aspects of Lewis's works that shed light on his further spiritual journey.

Something seems to have happened in the writing of *The Pilgrim's Regress*, as works of all types seemed to literally flow from Jack's pen afterward—works which were well received by critics and by the audiences they were intended for.

Again, we turn to Owen Barfield. In his introduction for *Light on C. S. Lewis*, Barfield describes the explosion in both the quantity and the quality of Jack's literary output after 1933.

> I had written and published two books which, in their limited sphere, could both be regarded as successes. He on the other hand had only *Spirits in Bondage* and *Dymer* to his credit, and, if my puny sales were only in four figures, his were still in three. This remained the position until *The Pilgrim's Regress* . . . after which he never looked back, but appeared to my dazzled eyes to go on for the rest of his life writing more and more successful books at shorter and shorter intervals. (xii–xiii)

On February 18, 1938, Tolkien wrote a letter to Stanley Unwin, whose firm, Allen and Unwin, had published *The Hobbit* six months earlier. In it Tolkien briefly mentions the sequel which he had started on, but his main purpose in the letter is to praise a book a friend had written.

> Mr. C. S. Lewis tells me that you have allowed him to submit to you "Out of the Silent Planet." I read it, of course; and I have since heard it pass a rather different test: that of being read aloud to our local club (which goes in for reading things short and long aloud). It proved an exciting serial, and was highly approved. But of course we are all rather like-minded. (29)

Tolkien goes on to explain that for some time he and Lewis had been working on parallel tasks. Lewis was to write a space-travel story, and Tolkien a story involving time travel. "The Space-journey has been finished," Tolkien concludes. "The Time-journey remains owing to my slowness and uncertainty only a fragment."

Sometime in 1937, Lewis and Tolkien had discussed—and lamented— the kind of stories that were being published. In the end, they decided that if they wanted more of the kind of books they liked, they would simply have to write them themselves. Tolkien suggests in a July 16, 1964, letter that the two men actually tossed a coin to see which genre—time travel or space travel—each would take. Tolkien's time-travel story, a piece titled "The Lost Road," was never completed. Lewis's space-travel story would be finished and on the bookstore shelves the next year.

Despite Tolkien's letter of praise, Allen and Unwin passed on Jack's new book. It was quickly picked up by the London publishing firm The Bodley Head and was published on September 23, 1938.

Out of the Silent Planet tells the story of a Cambridge philologist named Elwin Ransom, a character loosely based on Tolkien, who is kidnapped while on a walking trip and taken to the planet Mars, where, in the end, he meets the archangelic creature who governs the planet. In the novel's final chapter, the narrator suddenly states, "It is time to remove the mask and to acquaint the reader with the real and practical purpose for which this book has been written" (150). Lewis then introduces himself as the storyteller of Ransom's unbelievable but purportedly true tale. "It was Dr. Ransom," the Lewis character explains, "who first saw that our only chance was to publish in the form of *fiction* what would certainly not be listened to as fact. He even thought—greatly overrating my literary powers—that this might have the incidental advantage of reaching a wider public" (152).

In this attempt "to publish in the form of *fiction* what would certainly not be listened to as fact," Lewis had found his literary way. And in the process he had invented a new creative genre—one he would excel in.

Woven into the tale of space travel to Mars is a semiveiled account of Satan's rebellion, angelic warfare, the fall of man, and Christ's redemption. This scheme of smuggling in theology under the guise of fiction would become Lewis's formula not only for *Perelandra* and *That Hideous Strength*, the following two books in his Space Trilogy, but for his remaining fictional output. As David Downing points out in *Planets in Peril*, Lewis's goal was to use fiction to plant in readers' imaginations the suggestion that "there may be more things in heaven and earth than are dreamt of in their philosophies" (34).

So did Lewis's theological fiction reach a wider public than his straightforward apologetic works? When we think of works still to come such as *The Screwtape Letters* or the Chronicles of Narnia, we might be tempted to answer yes. But we might pause when considering a work like *Mere Christianity*, which has reached a very wide audience that includes not only all denominations of Christians but many nonbelievers as well.

Could we say that Lewis's fictional works and his apologetic works reach *different* audiences? Possibly, although many readers enjoy both types of Lewis's writing.

Perhaps the most accurate statement would be that Lewis's apologetic writing and his theological fiction, the kind of writing he undertook in *Out of the Silent Planet*, affect readers in different ways: his apologetics appealing to their heads, his fiction to their imagination and hearts.

If 1938 marked the beginning of Jack's new style of fictional output, 1940 marked the beginning of his long string of apologetic writing—one that would include more theological works such as *Miracles* (1947) and *Mere Christianity* (1952), as well as books with a more devotional tone such as *Reflections on the Psalms* (1958) and *Letters to Malcolm* (1964).

If Jack had found his fictional way in *Out of the Silent Planet*, he found his nonfictional way next with *The Problem of Pain*. It is here that we find for the first time Lewis's trademark style of apologetics, a style that respects the intelligence of his readers while speaking to them in a way that avoids jargon and is easy to understand; a style that is winsome, compelling, and, most of all, highly personable. In reading Lewis's engaging mix of explanation, clarification, evidence, example, comparison, and argument, it is almost as if a friend—an extraordinarily well-spoken and persuasive friend—were in the same room speaking to us.

In the years to come, Lewis's apologetic writing would become widely popular with readers of all sorts. But he sometimes also met with criticism, some of it fierce, from professional theologians who thought his use of everyday language oversimplified the complex doctrines he was trying to explain. Lewis typically did not respond to these attacks, but in 1958 he published a "Rejoinder to Dr. Pittenger" to explain why his apologetic works took the form they did.

> When I began, Christianity came before the great mass of my unbelieving fellow-countrymen either in the highly emotional form offered by revivalists or in the unintelligible language of highly cultured clergymen. Most men were reached by neither. My task was therefore simply that of a *translator*—one turning Christian doctrine, or what he believed to be such, into the vernacular, into language that unscholarly people would attend to and could understand. (183)

Perhaps Lewis had grown tired of the kind of professional clergymen and doctors of theology who were so caught up in their own narrow, academic treatises that they forgot ordinary believers and disdained anyone who did not share their educational superiority. For we can hear his frustration as he concludes his rejoinder by turning the tables on Dr. Pittenger and his colleagues.

> What methods, and with what success, does he employ when he is trying to convert the great mass of storekeepers, lawyers, realtors, morticians, policemen and artisans who surround him in his own city? One thing at least is sure. If the real theologians had tackled this laborious work of translation about a hundred years ago, when they began to lose touch with the people (for whom Christ died), there would have been no place for me. (183)

Unlike those professional theologians who found fault with Lewis's writing, publisher Ashley Sampson had read and was impressed by *The Pilgrim's Regress* and *Out of the Silent Planet* and asked whether Lewis would be willing to write a book on pain for the Christian Challenge series he was editing. Jack's first response was to ask whether he might write it but not publish it under his name, as he explains in the preface which copies of *The Problem of Pain* still bear today:

> When Mr. Ashley Sampson suggested to me the writing of this book, I asked leave to be allowed to write it anonymously, since, if I were to say what I really thought about pain, I should be forced to make statements of such apparent fortitude that they would become ridiculous if anyone knew who made them. Anonymity was rejected as inconsistent with the series; but Mr. Sampson pointed out that I could write a preface explaining that I did not live up to my own principles! . . . I have never for one moment been in a state of mind to which even the imagination of serious pain was less than intolerable. If any man is safe from the danger of under-estimating this adversary, I am that man. (9–10)

Lewis goes on to state that any real theologian would quickly see that *The Problem of Pain* was the work of a layman and an amateur.

Some would say that Lewis's status as a layman was an essential asset to his apologetic works rather than the liability he seems to suggest it was. And while Jack was not a professional theologian, with his first class degree in philosophy from one of the most rigorous universities in the world, he was hardly an amateur. We might also note that the Inklings, who listened to, critiqued, and helped refine Jack's book, were experts of another sort.

Lewis opens chapter 2 of *The Problem of Pain* with these words:

> "If God were good, He would wish to make His creatures perfectly happy, and if God were almighty, he would be able to do what He wished. But the creatures are not happy. Therefore God lacks either goodness, or power, or both." This is the problem of pain, in its simplest form. (23)

And with these words, Lewis introduces the question of how, in a world of appalling suffering, can we believe in a God who is good. It is a question that had plagued thinkers down through the centuries, and one that was especially worth asking as, day by day, World War II increased in size and ferocity.

In a slender 144-page book, Lewis made his own attempt to reconcile human suffering and divine compassion and show how belief in a loving heavenly Father was still possible despite the misery we find all around us. Lewis not only carefully and methodically walks readers through a knotty theological discussion but also brings them, some for the first time, into the world of ideas and invites them to join the great conversation.

With all the pain in the world, how can we say God is all-powerful and all-loving? Lewis's solution was for us to reconsider what we mean by all-powerful and all-loving.

Lewis points out that much of the suffering in the world stems from free will, which includes the possibility for its abuse, the choice to harm instead of help. Yes, God is omnipotent, Lewis argues, but this does not mean he can "give a creature free will and at the same time withhold free will from it" (25). This was not a glib, abstract statement for Jack. Having lived through the atrocities of trench warfare, he was well acquainted with the ways, the means, and the extent to which people could and did choose to harm their fellow human beings.

Why does God permit his creatures to inflict this suffering on others? With clear and concrete illustrations, Lewis asks us to consider a God who intervened in the world and stopped any injury midprocess.

> We can, perhaps, conceive of a world in which God corrected the results of free will by His creatures at every moment. So that a wooden beam became soft as grass when it was used as a weapon, and the air refused to obey me if I attempted to set up in it the sound waves that carry lies or insults. But such a world would be one in which wrong actions were impossible, and in which, therefore, freedom of the will would be void. (30)

And, of course, much of our suffering is self-inflicted, caused by our own harmful choices. But a God who stopped us from harming ourselves could not be said to have given us free will.

But what about the suffering which cannot be traced to the exercise of free will—suffering which is not caused by our own choices or the choices of others? Lewis is not afraid to suggest that some of this suffering comes to us from God, from a God who loves us with an extreme love that is far deeper than mere kindness. In chapter 6 of *The Problem of Pain*, we find Lewis's famous declaration: "Pain insists on being attended to. God whispers to us in our pleasures, speaks in our conscience, but shouts in our pains: it is His megaphone to rouse a deaf world" (83).

What we want, Lewis argues, is not a loving Father in heaven who will not be satisfied with us until he has made us into a divine work of art, but a kindly, somewhat senile Grandfather in heaven who simply wants us to be happy and have a good time. We may wish that we were so unimportant to God that he would leave us alone to follow our own natural tendencies. We may wish God would stop trying to rouse us and make us into something far greater and grander. But in this desire, Lewis claims, we are asking God not to love us more but to love us less. Though we may wish for a less arduous destiny, God has other plans.

Lewis offers this powerful conclusion:

> God, who has made us, knows what we are and that our happiness lies in Him. Yet we will not seek it in Him as long as He leaves us any other resort where it can even plausibly be looked for. While what we call "our own life" remains agreeable we will not surrender it to Him. What then can God do in our interests but make "our own life" less agreeable to us, and take away the plausible sources of false happiness? (85–86)

The idea of being made perfect through suffering was not new with Lewis. Pointing to Hebrews 2:10, he notes that it is an old Christian doctrine. Lewis succeeds in presenting this concept in a way that is not only understandable by ordinary Christians but also embraceable. Quoting the poet Keats, Lewis argues that this world of suffering is in reality a "vale of soul-making" and concludes that "it seems on the whole to be doing its work" (97).

The Problem of Pain was published in October 1940. A little less than four months later, Jack received a letter from a correspondent whose name was unfamiliar to him.

"Dear Mr. Lewis," the letter began, "I address you by name because, although we have never met, you cannot be a stranger after allowing me—and many others—to know some of your thoughts and convictions in your book *The Problem of Pain*" (*CLII*, 469).

The letter was from James Welch, the director of religious broadcasting for the BBC. It would mark another turning point in Jack's Christian output.

"I write to ask whether you would be willing to help us in our work of religious broadcasting," Welch continues. "The microphone is a limiting, and rather irritating, instrument, but the quality of thinking and depth of conviction which I find in your book ought sure to be shared with a great many other people; and for any talk we can be sure of a fairly intelligent audience of more than a million" (*CLII*, 469–70).

Welch suggested two possible topics. The first was for Jack to speak about "the Christian, or lack of Christian, assumptions underlying modern literature" (*CLII*, 470). The other topic Welch proposed was a series of talks on "something like 'The Christian Faith as I See It—by a Layman.'"

On February 10, 1941, Lewis wrote back thanking Welch for his kind remarks. Noting that the first topic about modern literature did not suit him, Jack agreed to try his hand at the second.

Biographers Green and Hooper argue that the wartime talks on the BBC, later published as individual series and then collected as *Mere Christianity*, were "one of the most successful works that Lewis ever undertook" (246). One of the reasons for this success—besides, as it turned out, the way Lewis perfectly adapted his lecture voice for radio—was Lewis's very conscious decision to focus on those beliefs shared by all Christians in all times. Green and Hooper summarize Lewis's intentions: "Almost as soon as he became a Christian he found that many of his co-religionists were far more interested in talking about *differences* between Christians than what they had *in common*.

Lewis seems to have made up his mind almost at once not to be drawn into what he saw as fruitless controversy."

Though Lewis would have a number of great successes in life—including his breakout success with *The Screwtape Letters* a year later and the Chronicles of Narnia a decade after that—Hooper and Green conclude, "The clarity of Lewis's thought, his ability to encapsulate a great many facts into a few words, is perhaps nowhere better illustrated than in these broadcasts" (253).

Of course, what is missing from this account of Lewis's wartime broadcasts is the effect they had on the country at a time when encouragement was greatly needed. The opening words of the trailer for the film *The Lion Awakes* give a sense of what hearing Lewis's voice—which, after Churchill's, was the most recognized voice at the time—meant to those who tuned in. The dramatic trailer begins with these words: "In 1941, London was attacked for seventy-six consecutive nights. Bombs fell like black rain from the evening sky. In Britain's darkest hour, the BBC turned to the most unlikely of men to address his nation and add hope when all hope seemed lost."

George Sayer offers a personal recollection of what it was like to hear Lewis speak over the radio.

> His rich voice, educated yet earthy, came across perfectly. The extraordinary vitality that was characteristic of his best Oxford lectures made an unforgettable impression on almost everyone who listened, Christians and unbelievers alike. I remember being at a pub filled with soldiers on one Wednesday evening. At a quarter to eight, the bartender turned the radio up for Lewis. "You listen to this bloke," he shouted. "He's really worth listening to." And those soldiers did listen attentively for the entire fifteen minutes. (277–78)

It was around this same time that Jack preached "The Weight of Glory" at the University Church of St. Mary the Virgin in

Oxford—a sermon which in the years to come would frequently be listed among the best sermons of all time. With *The Problem of Pain*, his talks on the BBC, and "The Weight of Glory," we could say that the first half of the 1940s was immensely productive for Jack. And in addition to these, during this time Jack also wrote *A Preface to Paradise Lost* and *The Abolition of Man*—works which would by themselves be enough to distinguish any writer.

Yet there was one success that would outreach all these others. "My dear Wormwood."

On May 2, 1941, British readers opened *The Guardian*, a weekly Anglican religious newspaper, to find the first in a series of thirty-one strange letters that would arrive in weekly installments, claiming to have been written by a senior devil named Screwtape to his nephew, a novice tempter named Wormwood. When the entire collection was published in Britain in 1942 and in the States a year later, *The Screwtape Letters* became, as Alan Jacobs notes, Lewis's "first truly popular book" (161). It would propel him to international fame, eventually landing him on the cover of *Time* magazine on September 8, 1947, where he was pictured with a little devil on one shoulder.

The *Time* cover story, "Don versus Devil," a reference to Lewis's position at Oxford, notes that by 1947 all of Lewis's books added together had sold something over a million copies.

Today that number is over 200 million, and the number of copies of *Screwtape* alone stands at many million.

The origin of this series of devilish epistles is mentioned in a letter Jack wrote to Warnie on July 20, 1940.

> I have been to Church for the first time for many weeks owing to the illness. . . . Before the service was over—one could wish these things came more seasonably—I was struck by an idea for a book which I think might be both useful and entertaining. It would be called *As One Devil to Another* and would consist of

letters from an elderly retired devil to a young devil who has just started work on his first "patient." The idea would be to give all the psychology of temptation from the other point of view. (*CLII*, 426–27)

In a delightful phrase in his memoir, Warnie reports that *The Screwtape Letters* was the first of Jack's books to have the kind of broad public success that "brings money rolling in" (41). As this money began rolling in, Jack felt the need to give most of it away, and with the help of Owen Barfield, who served as his solicitor, he set up a charitable trust where two-thirds of his royalties automatically went to helping those in need.

In the preface to the 1960 edition of *The Screwtape Letters*, Lewis confesses: "Though I had never written anything more easily, I never wrote with less enjoyment. . . . The work into which I had to project myself while I spoke through Screwtape was all dust, grit, thirst, and itch. Every trace of beauty, freshness, and geniality had to be excluded" (xiv).

Though Lewis reports that *Screwtape* was suffocating to write, it remains a wonderfully uplifting book to read. As Mark DeForrest has rightly pointed out: "Despite the impressive array of tactics used by the forces of darkness, Lewis's book also bespeaks of the optimism of faith. . . . Despite the snares of Satan, the young man's faith in Christ triumphs over the forces of evil and, in this triumph serves as an example of the ordinary Christian running an extraordinary race of faith" (368).

Perhaps because it was the first of his books to gain large, international success, Lewis always seemed ready to poke fun at the notoriety that *The Screwtape Letters* enjoyed. In the 1960 preface, he refers to it as the kind of book that is given to god-children, the sort that "gravitates towards spare bedrooms, there to live a life of undisturbed tranquility in company with *The Road Mender, John Inglesant,* and *The Life of the Bee*" (vi). Lewis also recounts the story of the hospital worker preparing for job interviews who chose *Screwtape* from a list of books to read because "it was the shortest."

In the second half of the 1940s, the three C. S. Lewises described by Barfield—the literary critic, the fiction author, and the writer of Christian apologetics—continued down much the same path so successfully staked out in the first half of the decade. *That Hideous Strength* (1945) completed the Space Trilogy he had begun with *Out of the Silent Planet* and *Perelandra*. *The Great Divorce* (1946) was another fictional work through which Jack sought to justify the ways of God to man. *Miracles* (1947) became his most formal attempt to refute the naturalism he once embraced.

The three Lewises might have continued on this exact same path all through the 1950s and 1960s—writing these same kinds of books, seeing the same circle of friends, and living the same day-to-day life in Oxford—except for three major turnings, all of which came about unexpectedly. The first turning occurred when a great lion came bounding into Jack's dreams. Another began when he was passed over for a professor's chair. The third came when Jack befriended a displaced American divorcée and her two rambunctious children.

6

Husband, Widower,
and Brother Once More

(1 9 5 0 – 1 9 6 3)

How wicked it would be, if we could, to call the dead
back! She said not to me but to the chaplain, "I am at
peace with God." She smiled, but not at me.

—*A Grief Observed*, chapter 4

Famous Christian Author: The 1950s

In a letter dated December 20, 1951, Lewis writes to an American
friend, "I am going to be (if I live long enough) one of those
men who *was* a famous writer in his forties and dies unknown"
(*CLIII*, 150).

Jack was halfway serious about his diminishing fame, despite the fact that he had just seen the release of the second book in what looked like it might become a somewhat-successful series—but only moderately successful; nothing like what he had known in his forties.

The book Jack had just published was *Prince Caspian.* It followed *The Lion, the Witch and the Wardrobe*, which had come out twelve months earlier, in 1950. They would become the first installments in the Chronicles of Narnia—seven books that would be released one each year from 1950 to 1956 and would go on to outsell all of Lewis's other works combined.

Radio Times, a weekly magazine published by the BBC that provides television and radio program listings for the UK, briefly featured a four-page pullout supplement for children titled *Junior Radio Times*. It was there, on July 15, 1960—ten years after the release of *The Lion, the Witch and the Wardrobe*—that Lewis provided an account of how he came to write the Chronicles of Narnia. In a piece published under the headline "It All Began with a Picture," Lewis told the young readers:

> One thing I am sure of. All my seven Narnian books, and my three science-fiction books, began with seeing pictures in my head. At first they were not a story, just pictures. The *Lion* all began with a picture of a Faun carrying an umbrella and parcels in a snowy wood. The picture had been in my mind since I was about sixteen. Then one day when I was about forty, I said to myself: "Let's try to make a story about it."
>
> At first I had very little idea how the story would go. But then suddenly Aslan came bounding into it. I think I had been having a good many dreams of lions about that time. Apart from that, I don't know where the Lion came from or why He came. But once He was there He pulled the whole story together, and soon He pulled the six other Narnian stories in after Him. (53)

We have on record here that Lewis first attempted at age forty to turn this image of what would become Mr. Tumnus into a story. We may also have elsewhere a glimpse, but only that, from the time years before when the first pictures of Narnia initially came to him.

On November 17, 1914—twelve days before his sixteenth birthday—Jack wrote a letter to Arthur describing the early snowfall that had blanketed Great Bookham and Gastons, where he was living with the Kirkpatricks. With an allusion to Edvard Grieg's "March of the Dwarves," a musical piece Jack particularly enjoyed, he reported to Arthur on the snow.

> We have been deeply covered with it all week, and the pine wood near here, with the white masses on ground and trees, forms a beautiful sight. One almost expects a "march of dwarfs" to come dashing past! How I long to break away into a world where such things were true: this real, hard, dirty, Monday morning modern world stifles one. (*CLI*, 95)

In *C. S. Lewis: A Companion and Guide*, Walter Hooper provides the following paragraph, which was found on the back of one of Lewis's other manuscripts. These four sentences, penned by Jack in 1939 when he was about forty, are the first words he wrote for the story that would eventually become *The Lion, the Witch and the Wardrobe*, a work begun partly in response to a group of children who came to stay at the Kilns during the war.

> This book is about four children whose names were Ann, Martin, Rose and Peter. But it is mostly about Peter who was the youngest. They all had to go away from London suddenly because of the Air Raids, and because Father, who was in the army, had gone off to the war and Mother was doing some kind of war work. They were sent to stay with a relation of Mother's who was a very old Professor who lived by himself in the country. (402)

What Lewis does not mention in his piece for *Junior Radio Times* is that after trying to make the faun image into a story when he was forty, he got stuck. Really stuck. After writing just this one paragraph in 1939, he set the project aside and did not return to it for eight years. Then, around 1947, Jack started having dreams of the lion who pulled together not just this story but the other six as well.

Peter is the only character from this earliest start at the novel to make it into the later version of the story, where his age is reversed from youngest to oldest. Lewis kept the original number and gender for his protagonists—two girls and two boys. Unlike in the passage above, in *The Lion, the Witch and the Wardrobe* there is no indication that the Professor and the children are relatives. In fact, the old Professor is a rather mysterious stranger whom the Pevensie children have no connection with before going to stay at his home. Finally, if Lewis's original intention was to make the story "mostly about Peter who was the youngest," to some extent he kept this focus in the book's final form, where more attention is given to the youngest child, although this character is now Lucy.

While it is beyond the scope of this book to discuss all seven Chronicles in detail, readers interested in learning more can find excellent books about Narnia written by Jonathan Rogers, Paul Ford, Peter Schakel, Bruce Edwards, Marvin Hinten, and David Downing. The discussion below will point out a few key details, but the spiritual themes that Lewis weaves into these stories will be our focus.

Perhaps the first thing that must be said about the Narnia stories is what they are not. With *The Pilgrim's Regress* and "The Weight of Glory," we have seen that when he wanted to, Jack was able to write an allegory or a sermon.

The Chronicles of Narnia are neither.

In a letter written in 1958, Lewis contrasts his approach in the Chronicles of Narnia with Bunyan's approach in *The Pilgrim's Progress*.

> If Aslan represented the immaterial Deity in the same way in which Giant Despair represents Despair, he would be an allegorical figure. In reality however he is an invention giving an imaginary answer to the question, "What might Christ become like if there really were a world like Narnia and He chose to be incarnate and die and rise again in *that* world as He actually has done in ours?" This is not allegory at all. (*CLIII*, 1004)

In this same letter, Lewis gives a word for what he was trying to do in the Chronicles—not allegory but *supposal*.

Because this difference often confuses readers, Lewis clarified it in several letters, including one later published in *Letters to Children*. Again contrasting his work with Bunyan's, Lewis writes to a fifth-grade class in Maryland:

> You are mistaken when you think that everything in the books "represents" something in this world. Things do that in *The Pilgrim's Progress* but I'm not writing that way. I did not say to myself "let us represent Jesus as He really is in our world by a Lion in Narnia": I said "Let us *suppose* that there were a land like Narnia and that the Son of God, as He became a Man in our world, became a Lion there, and then imagine what would happen." If you think about it, you will see that it is quite a different thing. (44–45)

And so while Aslan is the answer to Lewis's supposal of what the Son of God might be like in a land like Narnia, the High King Peter is not meant to represent the apostle Peter, Edmund as a traitor does not represent Judas, and Lewis did not set out to have the White Witch be Pontius Pilate.

Perhaps the clearest expression of what Lewis hoped to do through the Narnia stories can be found in his essay "Sometimes

Fairy Stories May Say Best What's to Be Said." There Lewis explains that by casting spiritual truths into the imaginary world of Narnia, he hoped they could be freed of any off-putting "stained-glass and Sunday school associations" they might have been shackled with and thus could for the first time "appear in their real potency" (47). Referring to the barriers that instantly go up when some people hear words with any connection to the church, Lewis concludes: "Could one not thus steal past those watchful dragons? I thought one could."

Was Lewis successful in making Christian truths appear in their real potency? Fans all over the world will attest to the power of the Narnia stories. Among the most moving episodes are the account of Aslan's sacrifice for Edmund in *The Lion, the Witch and the Wardrobe*, the depiction of Narnia's creation in *The Magician's Nephew*, and the story of Narnia's end in *The Last Battle*.

Here are just a few of the spiritual truths that Lewis explores in the Chronicles of Narnia:

- Evil rarely appears as evil but usually comes disguised as something else.
- Help often comes in an unanticipated form—in a manner so strange that it may look like help only when looking back on it.
- Real community is made up of different types of individuals with different gifts and abilities.
- Celebration, joy, and merriment are central to life, not elements reserved only for holidays or vacations.
- The self-centered life is not glamorous, fun, or exciting but leads to death and destruction.
- The virtuous life is an adventure—but one that will involve hardship—and the only path leading to genuine happiness and true fulfillment.

In the Narnia stories, we also see the deep spiritual longing Lewis himself experienced in life. Besides Shasta's desire to travel to the North and his true home in *The Horse and His Boy* and Reepicheep's longing to reach Aslan's Country in *The Voyage of the Dawn Treader*, we also find this longing—this time fulfilled—in *The Last Battle* as the heroes of the seven Chronicles finally reach the land they have been looking for all their lives.

Later, in *Letters to Malcolm*, Lewis will propose that while the relation between God and a human being is more private and intimate than any relationship between two humans could ever be, there is also a far greater distance between the participants. He accuses Malcolm of making the relationship between God and man too snug and suggests that Malcolm's view needs to be supplemented by Revelation 1:17, where St. John reports that he fell at the feet of the risen Lord as one who was dead. Lewis goes on to write, "I think the 'low' church milieu that I grew up in did tend to be too cosily at ease in Zion" (13).

Throughout the Chronicles of Narnia, Lewis seeks to expand on the mere coziness that some Christians may feel toward God. In *The Lion, the Witch and the Wardrobe*, Mr. Beaver describes Aslan to the children: "Course he isn't safe. But he's good" (80). Several chapters later when the children actually meet Aslan, the narrator steps in to tell us, "People who have not been in Narnia sometimes think that a thing cannot be good and terrible at the same time" (126).

Here we find one of Lewis's greatest teachings. Christians who have an image of a God who is only good—as many do—need to be reminded that he is also terrible—or, we might say, terrifying. At the same time, those who have an image of a God who is only terrifying—as we have seen that Lewis himself did as a young believer—need to be reminded that he is good as well. Lewis's portrait of Aslan serves as a corrective to both errors.

One final testimony to the ability of the Chronicles of Narnia to present Christian truths in their real potency can be found in an exchange of letters Lewis had with the mother of a nine-year-old American boy named Laurence Krieg. Mrs. Krieg had written to Lewis about her son's concern that he loved Aslan more than Jesus. In Lewis's response, found in *Letters to Children*, he puts her fears to rest and also reveals some of his own intentions in creating the character of the great lion.

> Laurence can't *really* love Aslan more than Jesus, even if he feels that's what he is doing. For the things he loves Aslan for doing or saying are simply the things Jesus really did and said. So that when Laurence thinks he is loving Aslan, he is really loving Jesus: and perhaps loving Him more than he ever did before. (52)

While the Chronicles of Narnia dominated Lewis's literary output in the 1950s, there were many other noteworthy publications. The following list of books Lewis authored during this decade reveals an author who was still at the very top of his abilities and, despite his own assertion, far from finished being famous:

The Lion, the Witch and the Wardrobe (fairy tale, 1950)

Prince Caspian (fairy tale, 1951)

Mere Christianity (apologetics, 1952)

The Voyage of the Dawn Treader (fairy tale, 1953)

The Silver Chair (fairy tale, 1954)

The Horse and His Boy (fairy tale, 1954)

English Literature in the Sixteenth Century, Excluding Drama (literary criticism, 1954)

The Magician's Nephew (fairy tale, 1955)

Surprised by Joy (autobiography, 1955)

The Last Battle (fairy tale, 1956)

Till We Have Faces (fiction, 1958)

Reflections on the Psalms (apologetics, 1958)

Though the close, intense friendship between Lewis and Tolkien waned somewhat in the 1950s and 1960s, perhaps a comment from a letter Tolkien wrote in 1967, three years after Jack's death, may serve to summarize Lewis's literary achievement. Tolkien qualifies his statement, reminding his correspondent that neither of them liked *all* that they found in the other's fiction. He was particularly unimpressed by Lewis's Narnia books. But despite this, Tolkien declares, "The most lasting pleasure and reward for both of us has been that we provided one another with stories to hear or read that we really liked—in *large* parts" (378).

The first half of the 1950s brought one other professional accomplishment for Jack that is worthy of note. After being passed over for a professorship at Oxford not once but twice—in part due to his choice to write publicly about his faith—Lewis was offered the Chair of Medieval and Renaissance Literature at Cambridge, a much better position, which Tolkien convinced him to accept. On December 29, 1954, Jack gave his inaugural lecture to a standing-room-only audience. He remained a professor at Cambridge until his retirement in 1963, staying at his new college, Magdalene, during the week and at the Kilns on weekends and holidays.

The Fan from America, Two Weddings, and a Funeral

In 1965, Jocelyn Gibb, who had been Jack's friend and publisher, put together a book of essays titled *Light on C. S. Lewis*. The contributors, who had all known Lewis personally, were asked to comment on what sort of man he was. In his essay, "The Approach to English," Neville Coghill tells of an occasion where

Jack confessed to him, "I never expected to have, in my sixties, the happiness that passed me by in my twenties" (63). Jack had invited his old friend to have lunch at Merton College. The comment came as they saw Jack's wife, Joy, across the grassy quadrangle.

It is safe to say *no one* anticipated the happiness that the aging, bachelor don from Belfast and the Jewish American divor-cée from the Bronx—sixteen years his junior, a former member of the Communist Party, and a recent convert to Christianity—were to bring each other.

Nor did anyone anticipate the grief Jack would have in his sixties—the anguish that came following Joy's death.

In a letter he wrote from the Kirkpatricks' house on October 12, 1915, Jack told Arthur Greeves: "You ask me whether I have ever been in love: fool as I am, I am not quite such a fool as all that. . . . But though I have no personal experience of the thing they call love, I have what is better—the experience of Sappho, of Euripides, of Catullus, of Shakespeare, of Spenser, of Austen, of Bronte, of, of—anyone else I have read" (*CLI*, 146). Four de-cades later, this all changed. In his late fifties, Jack gladly became love's fool and experienced love personally—and found it to be infinitely better than just reading about the experience of others.

Joy and Jack's full story has been told in a number of places. Readers interested in learning more might enjoy the fine books written on the subject by Brian Sibley, Lyle Dorsett, and Douglas Gresham. Joy and Jack's story has also received a semihistorical treatment in *Shadowlands*, which was first a BBC television film starring Joss Ackland and Claire Bloom, then a stage play, and finally a major motion picture with Anthony Hopkins playing Jack and Debra Winger starring as Joy.

Lewis's experience late in life of a great love and a great loss had a profound effect on his spiritual journey, and so several aspects of it bear looking into here.

In the foreword he wrote for *Jack's Life*, Christopher Mitchell notes that the Hollywood film *Shadowlands* gives the impression that, before meeting Joy, Lewis had no contact with women and little experience of deep emotions. Mitchell rightly points out:

> One of the most persistent misperceptions about the man C. S. Lewis is that for the greater part of his life he lived safely cloistered away from the typical cares and burdens of normal everyday life. . . . According to the movie, it is not until Joy Gresham comes into his life that he is thrust out from underneath the shadows of Oxford's spires into the bright light of real living. Such a portrayal is troubling simply because it is not true. (iv)

That said, the time that Lewis had with Joy undoubtedly provided him with a depth of love he had never known before. In *A Grief Observed*, Lewis reports that during their time together they "feasted on love, every mode of it—solemn and merry, romantic and realistic, sometimes as dramatic as a thunderstorm, sometimes as comfortable and unemphatic as putting on your soft slippers" (23–24).

The definitive three-volume set of Jack's letters, *The Collected Letters of C. S. Lewis*, totals nearly four thousand pages. Edited by Walter Hooper and released in successive volumes between 2000 and 2007, the series greatly adds to the material available in the earlier *Letters of C. S. Lewis*, which came out in 1966. Of the thousands of letters Hooper provides in the three massive volumes, many of them available for the first time, there is a very special one that is missing. Actually, there are two letters that would be wonderful to have.

On January 10, 1950—we know this was the date because Warnie mentions it after the fact in his diary—Jack received his first letter from an American fan who signed her name as Mrs. W. L. Gresham. After receiving this letter, Jack wrote her back.

While we do not have either of these letters, we do have one that Joy dashed off to Chad Walsh on January 29, 1950. Walsh had previously encouraged her to write Jack with some points she had wanted to raise. In *Out of My Bone: The Letters of Joy Davidman*, we find Joy's reaction to receiving her first letter from Jack.

> Just got a letter from Lewis in the mail. I think I told you I'd raised an argument or two on some points? Lord, he knocked my props out from under me unerringly; one shot to a pigeon. I haven't a scrap of my case left. And what's more, I've seldom enjoyed anything more. Being disposed of so neatly by a master of debate, all fair and square—it seems to be one of the great pleasures of life, though I'd never have suspected it in my arrogant youth. I suppose it's *unfair* tricks of arguments that leave wounds. But after the sort of thing that Lewis does, what I feel is a craftsman's joy at the sight of a superior performance. (116)

In this short passage we see aspects that would be characteristic of Joy—her quick wit, her love of heated discussion, and her passion for truth.

According to biographer Lyle Dorsett, Joy's first visit to England, in 1952, was made for a number of reasons: marital problems with her husband, Bill, who had a history of alcoholism and infidelity; a desire for time alone to complete the manuscript of a book she was working on; the need for physical rest after an extended illness; and her wish to meet the man whose writing had played an influential role in her conversion and with whom she had been corresponding.

Jack and Joy met for the first time on September 24, 1952, in the dining room of the Eastgate Hotel on Oxford's High Street. Joy had been staying in London with a friend and had invited Lewis to join the two of them for lunch. Lewis accepted and then returned the favor by inviting the two women to lunch in his rooms at Magdalen. George Sayer, who became the fourth member of this second meeting when Warnie withdrew, reports that the gathering was a "decided success" and remembers that there was stimulating conversation and roaring laughter (352).

Joy Davidman had made a favorable impression on Jack, and soon he asked her back to his college to meet Warnie and some of his colleagues. In his diary, Warnie notes that he found Joy to be "quite extraordinarily uninhibited" and records, "I was some little time in making up my mind about her" (273). Warnie goes on to say that during Joy's initial visit to England, the three of them had "many merry days together" and a "rapid friendship developed"—and it is clear he is referring not just to Jack's friendship with Joy but his own as well. Warnie concludes by noting that when she left, it was with "common regrets, and a sincere hope that we would meet again."

The three friends did meet again, perhaps sooner than they had expected. While Joy was in England, her husband was having an affair with her cousin and had also begun drinking heavily again. In December 1953, Joy moved to England with her two young sons, David and Douglas. Her divorce was finalized the following August.

For reasons unknown, Joy was unable to renew her visitor's visa. Perhaps her former membership in the Communist Party had come up. Perhaps the authorities at the Home Office were concerned about her financial status—she was living cheaply, with sporadic child support. She was also receiving assistance from the charitable fund Lewis had established. Rather than see her and the boys return to a situation in the States that was uncertain at best, Jack proposed a civil marriage that would allow them to remain in England. On April 23, 1956, Joy and Jack were wed at the Oxford registry office. Jack saw this as a legal marriage of mercy, a formality, a matter of expediency and friendship—not the sacrament recognized by the church.

Jack told only a few close friends about the new legal arrangement—Tolkien was not one of them—and expected that both their lives would go on as before, with Joy continuing to live at the house she had rented on Old High Street in Headington.

But their lives did not go on as before. Gradually, it became clear that their love was not a formality. It continued to grow. Unfortunately, at the same time there was something else that was growing. Just six months later, Joy was admitted to the hospital after a fall where her leg bone simply gave out. She was informed that what she had was not just a broken femur but an advanced cancer which had spread throughout her body. Despite a series of operations, Joy's doctors gave her only a few weeks or months to live. She was forty-one.

Even without Joy's disease, it is likely that Jack would have eventually proposed for real. Her desperate condition helped him to see sooner what those close to them already knew: that he was a man as in love as a man could be. On March 21, 1957, Joy received what everyone thought was a dying wish. With Warnie and one of the nursing sisters as witnesses, she and Jack were married in her hospital room by the Reverend Peter Bide, one of Jack's former pupils. In the eyes of the church, they promised to be faithful in sickness and in health and to love and cherish one another until they were parted by death. As a priest, Bide had witnessed several cases of miraculous healing after he had laid hands on the sick and prayed for them. After administrating the sacraments of Holy Matrimony and Holy Communion, he offered a similar prayer on Joy's behalf.

The entry we find for this day in Warnie's diary records the following:

> One of the most painful days of my life. Sentence of death has been passed on Joy and the end is only a matter of time. But today she had one little gleam of happiness. . . . At 11 a.m. we

all gathered in Joy's room at the Wingfield—Bide, Jack, sister, and myself, communicated, and the marriage was celebrated. I found it heartrending, and especially Joy's eagerness for the pitiable consolation of dying under the same roof as Jack; though to feel pity for anyone so magnificently brave as Joy is almost an insult. She is to be moved here next week. . . . There seems little left to hope but that there may be no pain at the end. (274–75)

Several days later, Joy was carefully transported by ambulance to the Kilns. Declaring that there was nothing more they could do, her doctors had agreed she could be allowed to go home to die.

And then Jack—and all those praying for Joy—received the miracle that had not come fifty years earlier when a nine-year-old boy in Belfast had prayed for a similarly cancer-stricken mother. After recording the entry for March 21, 1957—perhaps because the sorrow was too great and the events that followed too marvelous—Warnie closed the cover on his diary, and we find a large gap. The next entry is dated November 13, 1958. After reading over the words he had set down eighteen months earlier, Warnie put pen to paper once more, writing: "The last entry makes curious reading now when Joy is busy in the kitchen cooking our dinner. A recovery which was in the truest sense a miracle—admitted to be such by the doctors" (275).

After being sent home to die, Joy instead began to recover—slowly but surely. And she continued to recover. In time, Joy was strong enough to walk with a cane. Then later, as noted by Warnie, she was up and cooking for the three of them. Soon Joy was overseeing a number of major repairs and redecoration projects at the Kilns, work that the brothers had put off for years.

Jack's account of what happened can be found in several places. In "The Efficacy of Prayer," published in January 1959, we find this semiveiled report:

I have stood by the bedside of a woman whose thighbone was eaten with cancer and who had thriving colonies of the disease in many other bones as well. It took three people to move her in bed. The doctors predicted a few months of life; the nurses (who often know better), a few weeks. A good man laid his hands on her and prayed. A year later the patient was walking (uphill, too, through rough woodland) and the man who took the last X-ray photos was saying, "These bones are as solid as rock. It's miraculous." (3–4)

In a letter written to his friend Sister Penelope on November 6, 1957, Lewis provides a more personal narrative, noting that when Joy was sent home, everyone believed she was close to death.

Then it began to appear that the cancer had been arrested: the diseased spots in the bones were no longer spreading or multiplying. Then the tide began to turn—they were disappearing. New bone was being made. And so little by little till the woman who could hardly be moved in bed can now walk about the house and into the garden—limping and with a stick, but walking. (*Letters of C. S. Lewis*, 470)

Lewis goes on to report that his own bones had started losing calcium "just about as fast as Joy was gaining it." Charles Williams had introduced Jack to the concept of Christian substitution, literally one Christian taking on and bearing the burdens of another. Lewis believed that God had allowed him to bear some of Joy's suffering. Though the osteoporosis that Jack developed during the time Joy was recovering became less painful, it was a condition that remained with him the rest of his life.

Following Joy's recovery, she and Jack experienced real happiness for the better part of two and a half years, taking trips to both Ireland and Greece—the former being the occasion for their first ride in an airplane, which, after a moment of initial terror, they both found exhilarating.

But Joy's cancer came back, and she died three months after the trip to Greece, on July 13, 1960. Following her wishes, the funeral was held at Oxford Crematorium, and her ashes were scattered in its garden. The service was conducted by the Reverend Austin Farrer. He and his wife, Kay, had been among the first friends Joy made after moving to Oxford, and it was they who had gotten Joy to the hospital the night her leg had snapped. Now, as he and Kay stood alongside Jack, Warnie, Douglas, and David, Reverend Farrer offered words of gratitude from the Order for the Burial of the Dead found in the Book of Common Prayer.

"We give thee hearty thanks," Farrer prayed, "for that it hath pleased thee to deliver this our sister out of the miseries of this sinful world. . . ."

Joy's painful miseries were finally over.

In his memoir, Warnie offers a recollection of the woman who for a time became not only his sister-in-law but also a dear friend.

> For me, Jack's marriage meant that our home was enriched and enlivened by the presence of a witty, broad-minded, well-read and tolerant Christian, whom I had rarely heard equaled as a conversationalist and whose company was a never-ending source of enjoyment. . . . It would be an impertinence for me to compare my own sorrow at her death with his: nevertheless, I still continue to miss her sadly. (44–45)

Chapter 21 in George Sayer's biography is titled "Inspired by Joy." There Sayer discusses four books that Joy not only inspired or helped refine but also, in some cases, helped edit and type: *Till We Have Faces*, *The Four Loves*, *Reflections on the Psalms*, and *A Grief Observed*. It is to this final work that we now turn to further trace Lewis's spiritual journey.

The title *A Grief Observed* is telling for a number of reasons. First, as Douglas Gresham tells us in the foreword, we should not overlook the indefinite article at the beginning of the title indicating that these are the observations of one man's specific grief, a real grief. Gresham points out that anything titled *Grief Observed* would have to be "so general and nonspecific as to be academic in its approach and thus of little use to anyone approaching or experiencing bereavement" (6). Second, this is a grief *observed*. In this slender volume, we do not have the *edited* or *revised* afterthoughts of someone long after grief has subsided, but the actual observations of someone as he experiences each of grief's agonizing stages.

"What many of us discover in this outpouring of anguish," Gresham concludes, "is that we know exactly what he is talking about. Those of us who have walked this same path, or are walking it as we read this book, find that we are not, after all, as alone as we thought" (15).

"No one ever told me that grief felt so like fear. I am not afraid, but the sensation is like being afraid. The same fluttering in the stomach, the same restlessness, the yawning. I keep on swallowing" (19). So begins Lewis's rawest and most heart-wrenching work.

No one ever told me that grief felt so like fear.

A Grief Observed opens with anguish. It will end on a very different note.

The facts behind the book's creation are well known. At times incapacitated by grief in the days immediately following Joy's death, Jack turned to recording his thoughts and feelings in a series of four examination books he found lying about the Kilns. Throughout his observations, he refers to Joy as H.— which stood for Helen, a first name she rarely used. When the fourth manuscript book was filled several weeks later, Lewis considered the project finished.

Though not originally intending to publish the writings but only intending to help himself come to terms with his bereavement, Lewis was convinced to publish his observations in 1961, though he did so anonymously under the pen name of N. W. Clerk. The initials came from the Anglo-Saxon *nat whilk*, which translates "I know not whom," and thus the full name conveys, "I know not which clerk wrote this." After Lewis's death, the publishers asked and received permission to release the book under Lewis's own name, knowing that by doing so it would reach and comfort more people.

The book's four sections reflect the four manuscript books. In the following passage from the start of chapter 4, Lewis tells something of his intentions and some of what he has learned:

> This is the fourth—and the last—empty ms. book I can find. . . . I resolve to let this limit my jottings. I *will not* start buying books for the purpose. In so far as this record was a defense against total collapse, a safety-valve, it has done some good. The other end I had in view turns out to have been based on a misunderstanding. I thought I could describe a *state*; make a map of sorrow. Sorrow, however, turns out to be not a state but a process. It needs not a map but a history, and if I don't stop writing that history at some quite arbitrary point, there's no reason why I should ever stop. There is something new to be chronicled every day. Grief is like a long valley, a winding valley where any bend may reveal a totally new landscape. (76)

In between Lewis's opening statement of how his grief felt so like fear and his statement here at the start of the fourth section that his writing has done some good, we find a record of anger, doubts, questions, and accusations—outbursts which, Lewis admits, were not thoughts so much as attempts to hit back. Again and again, we find Lewis disagreeing with some response he had just given voice to. For example, at the start of chapter 2 he writes: "For the first time I have looked back and read these notes. They appall me. From the way I've been talking anyone would think that H.'s death mattered chiefly for its effect on myself" (33). Toward the end of the chapter, he stops again and comments: "I wrote that last night. It was a yell rather than a thought" (47).

But Jack did not edit out his appalling statements or those passages where he was just yelling.

Long before the rest of the counseling world came to fully recognize the point, Lewis shows us that these responses are a valid and, for many, a *necessary* part of grieving and so must remain. In fact, one of the greatest contributions of Lewis's account of grief is its testimony that pain, anger, doubt, and despair are normal and natural reactions to loss, feelings that should not be denied or repressed but recognized, expressed, and lived through. Lewis demonstrates how no stage in the process can be ignored if one is to successfully make it through the process of grieving and come out the other side.

Two decades earlier, in *The Problem of Pain*, Lewis had written: "If God is wiser than we His judgment must differ from ours on many things, and not least on good and evil. What seems to us good may therefore not be good in His eyes, and what seems to us evil may not be evil" (33). But, Lewis continued, when we say that God is good, by *good* we cannot mean the complete reverse or something wholly other than what we normally mean.

"The Divine 'goodness' differs from ours," Lewis concluded, "but it is not sheerly different: it differs from ours not as white from black but as a perfect circle from a child's first attempt to draw a wheel" (35).

As Jack encountered and charted the pain of Joy's death, not as a theoretical or intellectual problem but one that confronted him personally and directly, his faith was put to the test. He did not question God's existence or that God was good—these he continued to affirm. Instead, he questioned the *quality* of this divine goodness. If God's goodness is such that it could not be discerned amid Joy's suffering and death and the anguish Jack felt, then what kind of goodness was it? Early in chapter 1 of *A Grief Observed*, Lewis writes:

> Meanwhile, where is God? . . . When you are happy, so happy
> that you have no sense of needing Him, so happy that you are
> tempted to feel His claims upon you as an interruption, if you
> remember yourself and turn to Him with gratitude and praise,
> you will be—or so it feels—welcomed with open arms. But go to
> Him when your need is desperate, when all other help is vain, and
> what do you find? A door slammed in your face, and a sound of
> bolting and double bolting on the inside. After that, silence. (22)

Throughout *A Grief Observed*, Lewis turns again and again
to metaphor as the only way to express his powerful feelings.
Here he feels as though God has retreated behind a shut and
locked door. In another place Lewis compares humans to rats
in a laboratory experiment. Later he wonders whether his faith
was only a house of cards that could be knocked down at the
first blow.

In chapter 3, Lewis comes to a turning point. As he wrestles
with God's sometimes-difficult-to-understand goodness, he
states, "But the real question is whether he is a vet or a vivisec-
tor" (57). Lewis notes that a cat—and he had owned a number
of them—will spit and growl and even try to bite back as the
veterinarian tries to administer the very treatment that is going
to deliver it from its ailments and bring about healing. The cat,
in its limited understanding, does not see that what the vet is
doing is for its good. This does not mean that the vet is not good.

In the end, Lewis did not lose his faith following Joy's death—
as some have claimed. In the end, he found a peace which was
comprehensible as well as a peace which passed understanding.

"You can't see anything properly while your eyes are blurred
with tears," Lewis concludes (63). The very intensity of the
anguish pulls down a heavy curtain. This is a concept Lewis

says he can make sense of. "I have gradually been coming to feel that the door is no longer shut and bolted," he goes on to note. "Was it my own frantic need that slammed it in my face?" Lewis suggests it was and that perhaps his yelling had drowned out the voice he was hoping to hear. He concludes, "You must have a capacity to receive, or even omnipotence can't give."

To this insight about grief—that a person must have a capacity to receive before God can give—Lewis adds another. Several pages later he records: "The notes have been about myself, and about H., and about God. In that order. The order and the proportions exactly what they ought not to have been" (79). If the way into grief began with a focus first on his own needs and his own pain, Lewis maintains that once this stage has passed, the way out must reverse this focus. Here, fifteen pages before the end of *A Grief Observed*, Lewis has come to the point where praise—not yelling or trying to hit back—has become the best source of relief. And this praise must take a certain form: first praise of God as the giver, and then praise of Joy as the gift. Lewis concludes, "I must do more of this."

This is not to say that his own needs are not to be considered at all. Lewis adds one further insight which may seem more commonplace but which the counseling world has come to see the validity of as well. He reports that his heart was feeling lighter than it had been for a number of weeks. Lewis attributes this lightening to simply paying better attention to his physical well-being: "I am recovering physically from a good deal of mere exhaustion," he notes after having a particularly healthy day and a sound night's sleep (62).

Near the end of *The Last Battle*, Tirian enters the stable only to find it is nothing like he expected. Instead of being in a small, dark, enclosing space, he finds himself on a wide, grassy plain bathed in light. A gentle breeze is blowing. And, perhaps most astonishing, Tirian hears a voice and turns around to discover he is surrounded by friends. By contrast, the dwarves who are also there are able to perceive none of this.

In the concluding chapter of *A Grief Observed*, Lewis tells of an experience quite similar to the one depicted in *The Last Battle*—with his own position being somewhere in between that of Tirian, who can see all that is there, and the dwarves, who can see nothing. Here, as in other times when Lewis describes a mystical experience, we must turn to his own words.

> One moment last night can be described in similes; otherwise it won't go into language at all. Imagine a man in total darkness. He thinks he is in a cellar or dungeon. Then there comes a sound. He thinks it might be a sound from far off—waves or wind-blown trees or cattle half a mile away. And if so, it proves he's not in a cellar, but free, in the open air. Or it may be a much smaller sound close at hand—a chuckle of laughter. And if so, there is a friend just beside him in the dark. Either way, a good, good sound. (81)

Jack did not lose his faith after Joy's death, but neither did he get all his questions answered. But it was in the way his questions about God's goodness, Joy's suffering, and his own pain were not answered that Jack came to a resolution. He explains:

> When I lay these questions before God I get no answer. But a rather special sort of "No answer." It is not the locked door. It is more like a silent, certainly not uncompassionate, gaze. As though He shook His head not in refusal but waiving the question. Like, "Peace, child, you don't understand." (86–87)

A page later, Lewis speculates that all his questions about the problem of pain ultimately will not be resolved by some subtle reconciliation between what seem to be contradictory notions. He senses instead that "some shattering and disarming simplicity is the real answer" (89).

Instead, Lewis proposes, in the end we shall see that there never was any problem.

Earlier it was suggested that in the darkness of heartache that descended on Jack after Joy's death, he found himself in a position between that of Tirian and that of the dwarves. But in truth, Jack's position was much closer to Tirian's. Unlike the dwarves, Jack was aware that there was more to reality than he was able to perceive and that this something more was characterized by a great goodness.

In the final paragraph of *A Grief Observed*, Jack writes: "How wicked it would be, if we could, to call the dead back! She said not to me but to the chaplain, 'I am at peace with God.' She smiled, but not at me" (94).

And so Lewis's observations of a grief that initially felt so like fear end in peace—peace and an unlocked door, a compassionate gaze, a friend beside him in the dark, and a good, good sound like the sound of laughter.

In the serene acceptance we find at the end of *A Grief Observed*, Lewis also affirms the position he had described just months earlier in *The Four Loves*. There he explains:

> To love at all is to be vulnerable. Love anything, and your heart will certainly be wrung and possibly be broken. If you want to make sure of keeping it intact, you must give your heart to no one, not even to an animal. Wrap it carefully round with hobbies and little luxuries; avoid all entanglements; lock it up safe in the casket or coffin of your selfishness. But in that casket—safe, dark, motionless, airless—it will change. It will not be broken; it will become unbreakable, impenetrable, irredeemable. (121)

Lewis then concludes by charting the opposite course—not the safe path but our proper one: "We shall draw nearer to God, not by trying to avoid the sufferings inherent in all loves, but by accepting them and offering them to Him" (122).

And this is just what Jack did.

After telling us, "She smiled, but not at me," Lewis chooses to end *A Grief Observed* with a sentence taken from one of the final cantos of the *Paradiso*: "Poi si torno all' eternal fontana." Here Dante's beloved Beatrice turns away from him and towards the glory of God. *Then she turned back to the Eternal Fountain.* Jack finally lets go of his Helen Joy. But how is he able to do this? How is this even possible? Jack can let go because he knows, truly knows, that he is letting her go into the hands of God, who is the everlasting source of living water.

Earlier Lewis commented that his notes had been about himself, about Joy, and about God—in an order and proportion exactly the opposite of what they ought to have been. *Then she turned back to the Eternal Fountain.* Jack does not include himself in the final sentence at all. It begins with Joy and ends with God. Jack finally has the order right. And now that he has the order right, he can let go. This letting go, this acceptance of Joy's death, will not be an end to the burden of grief. But now the burden is bearable.

Brother Once More

In "Life After Joy," the final chapter of his biography, George Sayer reports that for a period of about eleven months—before Jack's own health began to fail—Jack's outward life in many ways returned to normal. There was work to do at Cambridge during the week, and weekends and holidays to spend at the Kilns with Warnie. There were still endless letters to answer and two books yet to write. During this period, Jack continued to make time for regular meetings with his Oxford friends. Sayer notes that Jack was now more willing than before to be dependent on these friends, more willing to accept invitations for lunch or dinner or for a drive in the country.

A Grief Observed was published in Britain in September 1961. Following close on its heels a month later was a book of literary scholarship, *An Experiment in Criticism*. Jack would write only one more book about his faith during his lifetime, and it would not come out until after his death.

In *C. S. Lewis: A Companion and Guide*, Walter Hooper includes part of a letter Jack received from Jocelyn Gibb dated June 13, 1963. Gibb had written to say the typed copy of Lewis's recently completed book had arrived. "This . . . has knocked me flat," Gibb declares. "Not quite; I can just sit up and shout hurrah, and again hurrah. It's the best you've done since *The Problem of Pain*. By Jove, this is something of a present to a publisher!" (380).

The book Gibb had received was *Letters to Malcolm*. As Hooper rightly notes, it is one of Lewis's "most outstanding works on Christian apologetics" (380).

Letters to Malcolm differs from Lewis's previous writing in several respects. First, although Hooper lists it among Lewis's apologetic works, with Lewis's creation of several imaginary characters—Malcolm; his wife, Betty; and their son, George—it is also a work of fiction, the only work where Lewis can be said to have combined reason and imagination in equal portions.

Second, if we exclude *A Grief Observed* from the list, *Letters to Malcolm* is also the only work where Lewis does not assume anything like the stance of an expert. In a letter to Gibb about the blurb that was to appear on the cover, Lewis requested, "I'd like you to make the point that the reader is merely being allowed to listen to two very ordinary laymen discussing the practical and speculative problems of prayer as these appear to them" (*CLIII*, 1434). Peter Schakel has proposed that Lewis's use of a letter format was strategically chosen to remove him from a position of authority: "He is not an 'expert' qualified to deliver talks on the BBC, or a scholar who has worked out a carefully reasoned defense of the possibility of miracle. These are just 'letters'" (175).

How, specifically, did Jack's experience of grief affect his writing in *Letters to Malcolm*? Alan Jacobs comments: "It is certainly different from his other books on Christianity, and the chief difference is the number of questions it contains: question marks are scattered through the book like confetti. He raises far more puzzles than he can solve—more, one might say, than he is inclined to solve" (292).

The abundance of questions throughout *Letters to Malcolm* reveals an openness Lewis now possessed in greater measure than before—a greater openness to mystery, a greater openness to ideas and opinions different from his own, and (to use Jewel's phrase in *The Last Battle*) a greater openness to take whatever adventure Aslan would send.

In the second letter, Lewis turns to a discussion of Rose Macaulay, the English author who was in the habit of collecting ready-made prayers, prayers which had been written by other people which she would then use for prayer herself. Lewis writes to Malcolm that although her method would not do for either of them, he is sure Macaulay's method was the right one for her.

"Broaden your mind, Malcolm," Lewis tells his fictional correspondent. "Broaden your mind! It takes all sorts to make a world; or a church" (10). He then uses the opportunity to launch into a description of a Greek Orthodox service he had attended.

> What pleased me most . . . was that there seemed to be no prescribed behavior for the congregation. Some stood, some knelt, some sat, some walked; one crawled about the floor like a caterpillar. And the beauty of it was that nobody took the slightest notice of what anyone else was doing. I wish we Anglicans would follow their example.

Lewis shows a different kind of openness in talking about the Lord's Supper in letter 19. When it comes to what happens in the moment of receiving the bread and wine, Lewis confesses to a complete lack of comprehension.

> However, then, it may be for others, for me the something that holds together and "informs" all the objects, words, and actions of this rite is unknown and unimaginable. I am not saying to anyone in the world, "Your explanation is wrong." I am saying, "Your explanation leaves the mystery for me still a mystery." (102–3)

Lewis makes it clear that he not only is comfortable with this mystery but also prefers to leave it this way. To do otherwise, for him, would be like taking a burning coal out of the fire to analyze it. The examination quickly turns a live coal into a dead one. Lewis points out, "The command, after all, was Take, eat: not Take, understand" (104).

On the final page of *Letters to Malcolm*, Lewis reveals that he would have no problem should any of his statements later be shown to be in error—and this is another kind of openness which he now embraced to a greater degree. "Guesses, of course, only guesses," he humbly writes. "If they are not true, something better will be" (124).

Writing the book just months before his death, Jack was at that time afflicted by osteoporosis, a weak heart, an enlarged prostate, and failing kidneys. There were occasions when he had to wear a corset-like surgical belt for his back and to use a catheter, as he put it, for the plumbing. For a time, he was also told he could not go up stairs. Later he was permitted to climb them but only at the slowest pace, or in bottom gear, as he put it.

Yet Lewis seemed to embrace it all as the adventure that was sent to him. He closes *Letters to Malcolm* in glad acceptance: "Thank Betty for her note," he tells the fictional Malcolm. "I'll come by the later train, the 3:40. And tell her not to bother about a bed on the ground floor, I can manage stairs again now, provided I take them 'in bottom.' Till Saturday" (124).

There would be just one more adventure for Jack. And he would accept this one as well.

Warnie writes near the end of his memoir that in these days of living at the Kilns after Joy's death, he felt as though the wheel had come full circle. It was not he, Jack, and Mrs. Moore—as it had been from the end of the Great War until 1950, when she was admitted to the nursing home. It was not he, Jack, and Joy—as it had been from their first days of friendship in late 1952 until her death eight years later. Now it was just he and Jack—together once more as they had been long ago in the little end room of the attic at Little Lea.

Warnie also reports that his brother faced his approaching death calmly and that his last weeks were not unhappy. "I have done all I wanted to do," Jack said to him one evening. "And I'm ready to go" (45).

Friday, November 22, 1963, began much like previous days, Warnie tells us, with breakfast, a few letters, and the morning crossword puzzle. After lunch, Jack fell asleep in his chair, and Warnie suggested that he would be more comfortable if he moved to the downstairs bed which had been set up for him. At four came tea and a few words between the brothers, and then, around five thirty, the end.

Epilogue

Home at Last

"I have come home at last! This is my real country! I belong here. This is the land I have been looking for all my life, though I never knew it till now."

—*The Last Battle*, chapter 15

A Flame That Did Not Flicker

Jack's funeral was held at Holy Trinity on November 26, and he was buried in the churchyard—just a few blocks from his home. Perhaps because President Kennedy had died the same day as Lewis, perhaps because in spite of his fame Jack had always remained a very private person, there were relatively few people at the service. Among them were Douglas and David Gresham, Tolkien and his son Christopher, Peter Bide, and George Sayer. Notably missing was Warnie, who had turned to the bottle to drown his sorrow. Also missing was a young American named Walter Hooper who had served as Jack's secretary over the summer and had promised to return after his teaching duties were over in January. Hooper did return in January, but now to serve as the editor of over a dozen of Lewis's books and, for five decades, to play a key role in keeping Lewis's work alive in print and available to future generations of readers all over the world.

George Sayer offers this account of the burial:

> We clustered around to see the coffin lowered into the grave. It was the sort of day Jack would have appreciated, cold but sunny. It was also very still. A lighted church candle was placed on the coffin, and its flame did not flicker. For more than one of us, that clear, bright candle flame seemed to symbolize Jack. He had been the light of our lives, ever steadfast in friendship. (410–11)

A week later, a memorial service was held in Oxford in the Magdalen College chapel, where Lewis had worshiped for many years. As he had at Joy's service nearly three and a half years earlier, Austin Farrer again offered words of comfort and remembrance.

Farrer commented that, as a writer, Lewis had a unique way of integrating his thoughts, emotions, and imagination—not compartmentalizing them—and that it was this "feeling intellect" and "intellectual imagination" that gave power to the many works Lewis had left behind (46). "There lived in his writings," Farrer told those who had come to honor their friend, teacher, and colleague, "a Christian universe which could be both thought and felt, in which he was at home, and in which he made his reader at home."

About Lewis the man, Farrer commented:

> His characteristic attitude to people in general was one of consideration and respect. He did his best for them and he appreciated them. He paid you the compliment of attending to

your words. . . . He was endlessly generous. He gave without stint, to all who seemed to care for them, the riches of his mind and the effort of his wit: and where there was need, he gave his money. . . . His patience and his loyalty were inexhaustible. He really was a Christian—by which I mean, he never thought he had the right to stop. (46–47)

Farrer ended with words of hope: "The life which Lewis lived with zest he surrendered with composure. He was put almost beside himself by his wife's death; he seemed easy at the approach of his own. He died at the last in a minute. May he everlastingly rejoice in the Mercy he sincerely trusted."

In his novels, Lewis had imagined a number of times what passing from this life to the next would be like. One of the most memorable is found in *The Voyage of the Dawn Treader*, where Reepicheep sails alone in his tiny boat up the great wave standing at the world's end. Lewis describes what happened next.

The coracle went more and more quickly, and beautifully it rushed up the wave's side. For one split second they saw its shape and Reepicheep's on the very top. Then it vanished, and since that moment no one can truly claim to have seen Reepicheep the Mouse. But my belief is that he came safe to Aslan's country and is alive there to this day. (244)

In *The Screwtape Letters*, Lewis imagined the passing to eternal life not from the point of view of those left behind but from the perspective of Wormwood's patient. At the moment of death, the man briefly sees Wormwood, who had been his tempter, but then sees the angelic host who had been assisting him all throughout his life. He feels for the first time a joy that is not fleeting and comes face-to-face with the risen Lord.

The dim consciousness of friends about him which had haunted his solitudes from infancy was now at last explained; that central music in every pure experience which had always just evaded memory was now at last recovered. Recognition made him free of their company almost before the limbs of his corpse became quiet. . . . He saw not only Them; he saw Him. (174)

Another equally moving passage can be found in chapter 15 of *The Last Battle*, where the ensemble cast find themselves in a strange new land, and Lewis has Jewel the Unicorn declare: "I have come home at last! This is my real country! I belong here. This is the land I have been looking for all my life, though I never knew it till now" (196).

But perhaps the most powerful words Lewis ever wrote about death and the eternal life that follows are the final sentences of *The Last Battle*. Adapted below, they serve as a fitting close for our exploration of Jack's spiritual journey.

> And for us this is the end of Jack's story, and we can most truly say that he lived happily ever after. But for Jack, it was only the beginning of the real story. All his life in this world and all his adventures on earth had only been the cover and the title page: now at last he was beginning Chapter One of the Great Story which no one on earth has read; which goes on forever: in which every chapter is better than the one before.

Looking for Lewis

My very first trip to Oxford came in my midthirties, after I received funding from my school to attend a summer seminar on British literature. Since then I have been back enough times that I have lost count—more than eight but less than twenty. That first seminar was based at Oriel College, which sits between Merton College, where Tolkien taught, and University College, where Jack had been a student. Like thousands of Lewis fans before me and thousands who have come since, I made the mandatory visits—people who don't understand what Lewis can mean to a life mockingly call them pilgrimages—to Magdalen College, the Eagle and Child, the Eastgate Hotel, the Kilns, and Holy Trinity, with several damaging stops in between at Blackwell's Bookshop.

On the plus side, Magdalen still looks very much as it must have looked to Lewis when he was a fellow there (and, we might be tempted to say, to Addison when he was a fellow in the early 1700s). You can look into the hall and see the high table where Lewis and his guests dined. You can stroll Addison's Walk and imagine the famous night when Jack walked and talked there with Tolkien and Dyson. Off to the side you can see Magdalen's famous deer park—still looking much as it did when Jack watched the small, mysterious animals from his back window. You can look inside the chapel, and, if your schedule permits, you can attend evensong and pray in the same stalls that Lewis prayed in and hear choral music which will sound exactly the same—and in some cases will be exactly the same—as when he was there.

If you ask at the porter's lodge, as I did, the porter will tell you how to find New Building (or "New Buildings," he may say) and the door to the staircase that leads up to Lewis's former rooms. I was reminded: "But you can't go up there. There's someone else there now."

And his statement speaks volumes.

If you go looking for Lewis at Magdalen (remember to pronounce it *maudlin*), you will find little evidence that from 1925 to 1954 C. S. Lewis was one of the college's most celebrated fellows and one of the university's most popular lecturers, or that fifty years after his death he remains one of the best-selling authors not just of Oxford but in the world. In the far corner of Addison's Walk, somewhat out of the way, you can find a stone plaque, erected in 1998 to commemorate the centenary of Lewis's birth, that features his lovely poem "What the Bird Said Early in the Year."

But that's about it.

On that first visit long ago, I asked my tutor why this was so. "Do you mean, why don't we have a C. S. Lewis snack bar, or little Lewis key chains for sale, or at least a glass display case with yellowed exam papers he had marked, one of his battered nib pens, and the tattered remnants of his gown?" he asked partially in jest—but only partially. My tutor answered his own question by telling me that Oxford had seen many great men come and go and would continue to do so. He reminded me that the university was already three hundred years old when Queen Elizabeth had visited—Elizabeth the First. "We would find that sort of veneration, which Americans are so prone to, well, rather vulgar," he added.

If it seems difficult to find much of Lewis at Magdalen, it is just the opposite at Holy Trinity. The unassuming parish church he attended for the thirty-some years after his conversion seems somehow a better fit to the unassuming man whose clothes were more shabby than natty and who looked more like a prosperous butcher than a celebrity. Inside, you can sit in the pew he shared with Warnie—and, for a time, with Joy. And you can pause to reflect that it was in this exact spot during a particularly dull sermon that Jack came up with the idea for *Screwtape*.

Listening to the wind in the trees of the churchyard where he and Warnie are buried, one senses a deep peace that is lacking down in the city. Despite the buildup that the village of Headington has seen, a good bit of the country remains at the grave of the man who loved his country walks. It is a rare day that someone has not left a flower on the gravestone or a bit of paper with thanks or a favorite quote. More recently, tiny Narnia action figures have started to appear from time to time—a little Aslan or a miniature centaur left behind to stand watch.

Of course, if you are looking for Lewis, the best place to find him is at the Kilns. Restored to look as it would have during the days when Jack and Warnie lived there—except much cleaner—the house welcomes visitors for tours by appointment, made through the C. S. Lewis Foundation, which owns and manages the property. Everyone I have talked to who has visited has found that a genuine sense of Lewis fills the rooms and the lovely garden as well.

Several years back, I was invited to lead one of the summer seminars-in-residence which the foundation hosts. During our week at the Kilns, we ate in its dining room, met for class in the library, held late-night conversations out in the common room, and slept in its bedrooms. I got to sleep in Jack's bedroom—as far as I can tell, the thing I have done in my life which has most impressed my mother.

As one can see in a picture of the Kilns, Jack's bedroom is located upstairs on the end toward the street, and a set of external stairs along the side of the house leads up to it. During our week, a plump, middle-aged cat, affectionately named Jack, wandered in every afternoon—from where no one knew for sure—to offer his greetings and inspect the grounds. I was warned that if the night was particularly cool and I left my window open, Jack had been known to climb up the balcony stairs looking for a warm spot at the foot of the bed.

Our week turned out to be especially cold, and I huddled beneath a triple layer of blankets each night with the window wide open, hoping for a visitor. Alas, neither the real Jack nor his namesake made an appearance during the nights I slept there.

In his book *Seeking the Secret Place: The Spiritual Formation of C. S. Lewis*, Lyle Dorsett reports that as Lewis was nearing death, Owen Barfield, who was serving as Lewis's legal advisor, asked him if he had decided how he wanted to allocate the future royalties from his books. In a statement which shows both his humility and the dubious value of predictions, Jack replied,

"After I've been dead five years, no one will read anything I've written" (20).

Given that Lewis's prediction was not merely incorrect but extravagantly so, I will hazard my own. If I am wrong, I will be in good company. And in any case, it is unlikely I will be around to be told I was wrong. Fifty years from now, at the one hundredth anniversary of Lewis's death, I believe people will still be reading and enjoying the Chronicles of Narnia, *The Screwtape Letters*, and *Mere Christianity* in great numbers. It is harder to predict which of his other books, Lewis's B-list, will still be popular. One contribution of digital and on-demand publishing is that all of Lewis's books are sure to be still available in some form five decades from now. It is hard to imagine that his lesser-known works will not continue to have avid and interested readers, though their numbers may not be as great as they are today.

Even if fifty years from now no one is actually reading Lewis, his writings would continue to bear fruit. His efforts to rediscover the Christian imagination, to reclaim Christian reason, and to restore a Christian vision of humanity live on in the minds and hearts of countless readers everywhere. The lives he touched are already affecting others, and they in turn are touching still more.

And after all is said, it is those lives which serve as the best measure of Lewis's accomplishment and are the best place for us to look for him—both now and in the years to come.

Bibliography

Augustine. *Confessions*. New York: Penguin, 1961.

Baker, Leo. "Near the Beginning." In *Remembering Lewis: Recollections of Those Who Knew Him*, edited by James Como, 65–75. San Francisco: Ignatius, 2005.

Barfield, Owen. Introduction to *Light on C. S. Lewis*, edited by Jocelyn Gibb, ix–xxi. New York: Harvest, 1976.

———. Preface to *The Taste of the Pineapple: Essay on C. S. Lewis as Reader, Critic, and Imaginative Writer*, edited by Bruce Edwards, 1–2. Bowling Green, OH: Bowling Green State Univ. Press, 1988.

Bleakley, David. *C. S. Lewis at Home in Ireland: A Centenary Biography*. Bangor, Northern Ireland: Strandtown Press, 1998.

Bramlett, Perry. "Prayer." In *The C. S. Lewis Readers' Encyclopedia*, edited by Jeffrey Schultz and John West, 331–33. Grand Rapids: Zondervan, 1998.

Bremer, John. "Clive Staples Lewis 1898–1963: A Brief Biography." In *The C. S. Lewis Readers' Encyclopedia*, edited by Jeffrey Schultz and John West, 9–65. Grand Rapids: Zondervan, 1998.

Chesterfield, Lord. *See* Stanhope, Philip Dormer.

Coghill, Neville. "The Approach to English." In *Light on C. S. Lewis*, edited by Jocelyn Gibb, 51–66. New York: Harvest, 1976.

Davidman, Joy. "The Longest Way Round." In *These Found the Way: Thirteen Converts to Protestant Christianity*, edited by David Soper, 13–26. Philadelphia: Westminster, 1951.

————. *Out of My Bone: The Letters of Joy Davidman*. Edited by Don King. Grand Rapids: Eerdmans, 2009.

DeForrest, Mark. "*The Screwtape Letters*." In *The C. S. Lewis Readers' Encyclopedia*, edited by Jeffrey Schultz and John West, 366–68. Grand Rapids: Zondervan, 1998.

Dorsett, Lyle. *Seeking the Secret Place: The Spiritual Formation of C. S. Lewis*. Grand Rapids: Brazos, 2004.

Downing, David. *Into the Region of Awe: Mysticism in C. S. Lewis*. Downers Grove, IL: InterVarsity, 2005.

————. *The Most Reluctant Convert: C. S. Lewis's Journey to Faith*. Downers Grove, IL: InterVarsity, 2002.

————. *Planets in Peril: A Critical Study of C. S. Lewis's Ransom Trilogy*. Amherst: Univ. of Massachusetts Press, 1992.

Duriez, Colin. *Tolkien and Lewis: The Gift of Friendship*. Mahwah, NJ: HiddenSpring, 2003.

Euripides. *Euripides: Four Plays in Modern Translations*. Translated by Simon Goldfield and Kenneth Cavander. New York: Dell, 1965.

Farrer, Austin. "In His Image: In Commemoration of C. S. Lewis." In *The Brink of Mystery*, edited by Charles Conti, 45–47. London: SPCK, 1976.

Glyer, Diana Pavlac. *The Company They Keep: C. S. Lewis and J. R. R. Tolkien as Writers in Community*. Kent, OH: Kent State Univ. Press, 2007.

Green, Roger Lancelyn, and Walter Hooper. C. S. *Lewis: A Biography*. London: HarperCollins, 2002.

Gresham, Douglas. Foreword to *A Grief Observed*, by C. S. Lewis, 5–16.

————. *Jack's Life: The Life Story of C. S. Lewis*. Nashville: Broadman & Holman, 2005.

Hooper, Walter. *C. S. Lewis: A Companion and Guide*. New York: HarperCollins, 1996.

————. Preface to *God in the Dock*, by C. S. Lewis, 7–17.

Jacobs, Alan. *The Narnian: The Life and Imagination of C. S. Lewis*. San Francisco: HarperSanFrancisco, 2005.

James, Richard. "Lewis's Early Schooling: Trials and Tribulations." In *C. S. Lewis: Life, Works, and Legacy*, edited by Bruce Edwards, vol. 1, *An Examined Life*, 45–78. Westport, CT: Praeger, 2007.

Kilby, Clyde. *The Christian World of C. S. Lewis*. Grand Rapids: Eerdmans, 1964.

Lewis, C. S. *All My Road Before Me: The Diary of C. S. Lewis, 1922–1927*. Orlando, FL: Harcourt, 1991.

————. "Answers to Questions on Christianity." In *God in the Dock*, 48–62.

————. "Christian Apologetics." In *God in the Dock*, 89–103.

————. *The Collected Letters of C. S. Lewis*. Edited by Walter Hooper. Vol. 1, *Family Letters, 1905–1931*. San Francisco: HarperSanFrancisco, 2004.

————. *The Collected Letters of C. S. Lewis*. Edited by Walter Hooper. Vol. 2, *Books, Broadcasts, and the War, 1931–1949*. San Francisco: Harper-SanFrancisco, 2004.

————. *The Collected Letters of C. S. Lewis*. Edited by Walter Hooper. Vol. 3, *Narnia, Cambridge, and Joy, 1950–1963*. San Francisco: HarperSan-Francisco, 2007.

————. "Cross Examination." In *God in the Dock*, 258–67.

————. "De Futilitate." In *Christian Reflections*, edited by Walter Hooper, 57–71. Grand Rapids: Eerdmans, 1995.

————. "The Efficacy of Prayer." In *The World's Last Night, and Other Essays*, 3–11. New York: Harvest, 1987.

————. *An Experiment in Criticism*. Cambridge: Cambridge Univ. Press, 1996.

————. *The Four Loves*. New York: Harvest, 1988.

————. *God in the Dock: Essays on Theology and Ethics*. Edited by Walter Hooper. Grand Rapids: Eerdmans, 1970.

————. *The Great Divorce*. New York: Touchstone, 1996.

————. *A Grief Observed*. New York: HarperSanFrancisco, 1994.

————. *The Horse and His Boy*. New York: Harper Trophy, 1994.

————. "Is Theology Poetry." In *The Weight of Glory and Other Addresses*, 141–57. San Francisco: HarperSanFrancisco, 2001.

————. "It All Began with a Picture . . ." In *On Stories, and Other Essays on Literature*, 53–54.

————. *The Last Battle*. New York: Harper Trophy, 1994.

————. *Letters of C. S. Lewis*. Edited by W. H. Lewis and Walter Hooper. New York: Harvest, 1993.

————. *Letters to an American Lady*. Grand Rapids: Eerdmans, 1971.

————. *Letters to Children*. Edited by Lyle W. Dorsett and Marjorie Lamp Mead. New York: Touchstone, 1995.

————. *Letters to Malcolm: Chiefly on Prayer*. New York: Harvest, 1992.

————. *The Lion, the Witch and the Wardrobe*. New York: Harper Trophy, 1994.

————. *The Magician's Nephew*. New York: Harper Trophy, 1994.

———. *Mere Christianity*. San Francisco: HarperSanFrancisco, 2001.

———. *Miracles*. New York: Touchstone, 1996.

———. 1960 preface to *The Screwtape Letters, with Screwtape Proposes a Toast*, rev. ed., v–xv. New York: Macmillan, 1982.

———. *On Stories, and Other Essays on Literature*. Edited by Walter Hooper. New York: Harvest, 1982.

———. "On Three Ways of Writing for Children." In *On Stories, and Other Essays on Literature*, 31–43.

———. *Out of the Silent Planet*. New York: Scribner, 2003.

———. *Perelandra*. New York: Scribner, 2003.

———. *The Pilgrim's Regress*. Grand Rapids: Eerdmans, 1992.

———. *Prince Caspian*. New York: Harper Trophy, 1994.

———. *The Problem of Pain*. New York: Touchstone, 1996.

———. *Reflections on the Psalms*. New York: Harvest, 1986.

———. "Rejoinder to Dr. Pittenger." In *God in the Dock*, 177–83.

———. *The Screwtape Letters*. New York: Touchstone, 1996.

———. *The Silver Chair*. New York: Harper Trophy, 1994.

———. "Sometimes Fairy Stories May Say Best What's to Be Said." In *On Stories, and Other Essays on Literature*, 45–48.

———. *Surprised by Joy*. New York: Harvest, 1955.

———. *That Hideous Strength*. New York: Scribner, 2003.

———. *The Voyage of the Dawn Treader*. New York: Harper Trophy, 1994.

———. "The Weight of Glory." In *The Weight of Glory and Other Addresses*, 25–46. San Francisco: HarperSanFrancisco, 2001.

Lewis, Warren. *Brothers and Friends: The Diaries of Major Warren Lewis*. Edited by Clyde Kilby and Marjorie Lamp Mead. New York: Ballantine, 1988.

———, ed. *The Lewis Papers: Memoirs of the Lewis Family, 1850–1930*. Oxford: privately printed, 1935. A typescript of the original is in the Wade Collection, Wheaton College, Wheaton, Illinois.

———. "Memoir of C. S. Lewis." In *Letters of C. S. Lewis*, 21–46.

MacDonald, George. *George MacDonald: An Anthology*. Edited by C. S. Lewis. New York: Touchstone, 1996.

———. *Unspoken Sermons*. New York: Cosimo, 2007.

———. *What's Mine's Mine*. Boston: D. Lothrop, 1886.

Milton, John. *Paradise Lost*. In *The Poetical Works of John Milton*, 103–390. Whitefish, MT: Kessinger, 2006.

Mitchell, Christopher. Foreword to *Jack's Life*, by Douglas Gresham, iv–vi.

Potter, Beatrix. *The Tale of Squirrel Nutkin*. London: Frederick Warne, 1903.

Sayer, George. *Jack: A Life of C. S. Lewis*. Wheaton: Crossway, 1994.

Schakel, Peter. *Reason and Imagination in C. S. Lewis: A Study of* Till We Have Faces. Grand Rapids: Eerdmans, 1984.

Shakespeare, William. *As You Like It*. Cambridge: Cambridge Univ. Press, 2009.

Smith, Stephen. "Awakening from the Enchantment of Worldliness: The Chronicles of Narnia as Pre-Apologetics." In *The Pilgrim's Guide: C. S. Lewis and the Art of Witness*, edited by David Mills, 168–84. Grand Rapids: Eerdmans, 1998.

Stanhope, Philip Dormer. *Letters to His Son*. Vol. 1. Whitefish, MT: Kessinger, 2005.

Tolkien, J. R. R. *The Letters of J. R. R. Tolkien*. Edited by Humphrey Carpenter. Boston: Houghton Mifflin, 2000.

Wagner, Richard. *C. S. Lewis and Narnia for Dummies*. Hoboken, NJ: Wiley, 2005.

White, Michael. *C. S. Lewis: The Boy Who Chronicled Narnia*. London: Abacus, 2005.

Wilson, A. N. *C. S. Lewis: A Biography*. London: Flamingo, 1991.

Yancey, Philip. *What Good Is God? In Search of a Faith That Matters*. Nashville: FaithWords, 2010.

Index

Devin Brown is a Lilly Scholar and professor of English at Asbury University. He is the author of number of books on Lewis and Tolkien. In summer 2008, he served as scholor-in-residence at the Kilns, Lewis's house outside Oxford. He and his wife, Sharon, live in Lexington, Kentucky with their 15-pound cat, Mr. Fluff.